EASY PIANO

A NEW MUSICAL

# WiCKED

MUSIC & LYRICS BY STEPHEN SCHWARTZ

www.stephenschwartz.com

ISBN 0-634-08793-2

HAL•LEONARD®
CORPORATION
7777 W. BLUEMOUND RD. P.O. BOX 13819 MILWAUKEE, WI 53213

In Australia Contact:
Hal Leonard Australia Pty. Ltd.
22 Taunton Drive    P.O. Box 5130
Cheltenham East, 3192  Victoria, Australia
Email:  ausadmin@halleonard.com

Visit Hal Leonard Online at
**www.halleonard.com**

# CONTENTS

# NO ONE MOURNS THE WICKED

Music and Lyrics by
STEPHEN SCHWARTZ

**Flowing, not too slow**

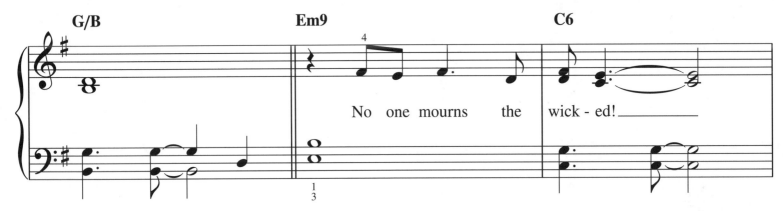

No one mourns the wick - ed! _____

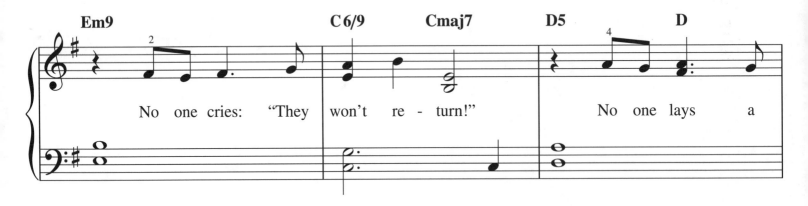

No one cries: "They won't re - turn!" No one lays a

lil - y on their grave! The good man scorns the

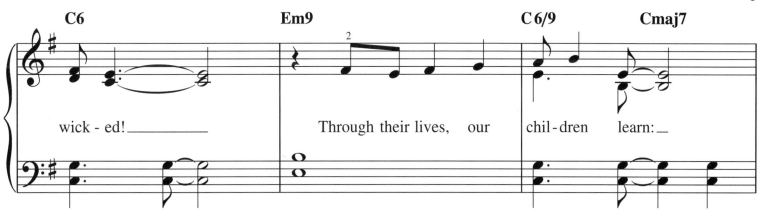

wick - ed! _____ Through their lives, our chil - dren learn: _

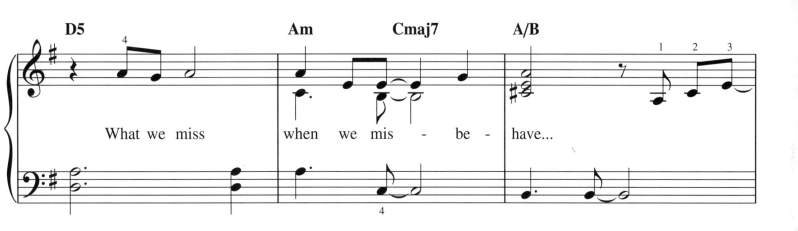

What we miss when we mis - be - have...

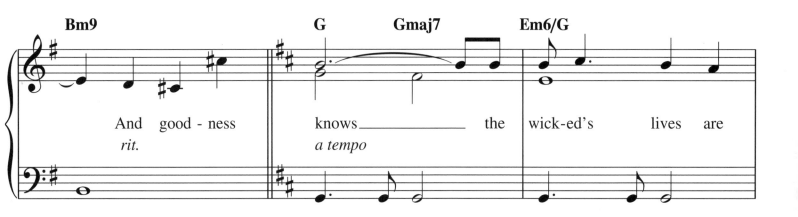

And good - ness knows _____ the wick-ed's lives are
*rit.* *a tempo*

lone - ly Good - ness knows _____ the

wick - ed   die   a - lone                                                                          It   just

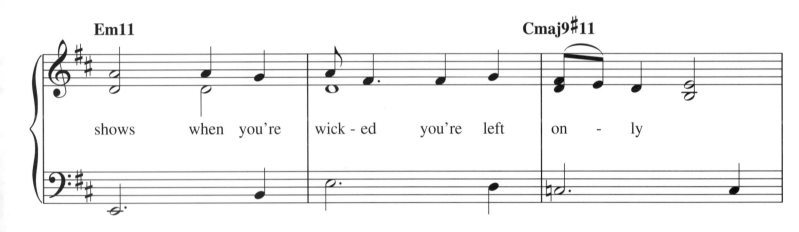

shows   when   you're   wick - ed   you're   left   on - ly

on   your   own...

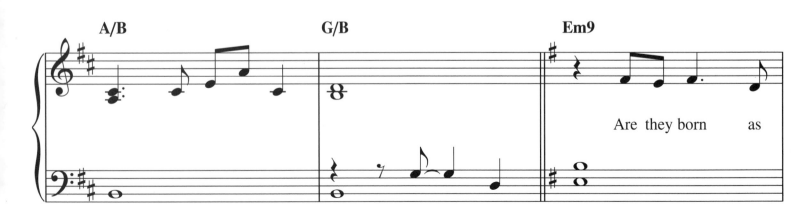

Are   they   born   as

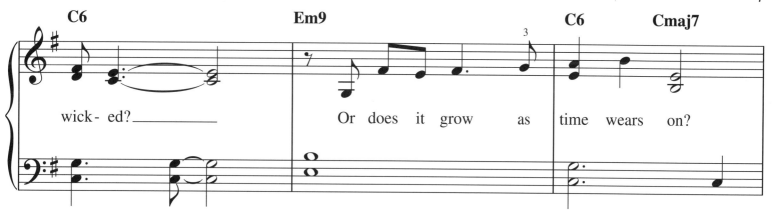

C6      Em9      C6    Cmaj7

wick- ed?_____ Or does it grow as time wears on?

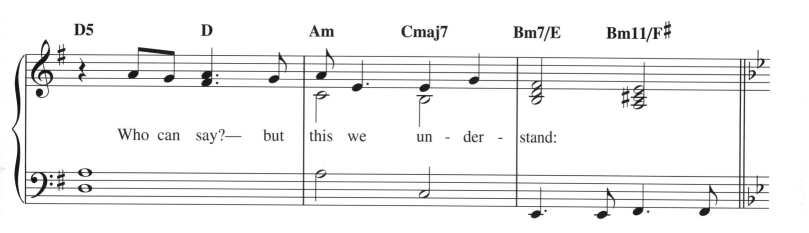

D5    D    Am   Cmaj7    Bm7/E   Bm11/F♯

Who can say?— but this we un-der - stand:

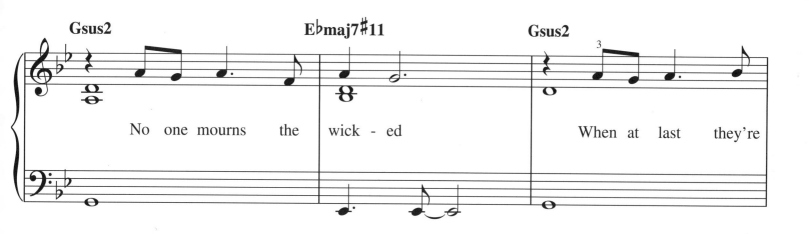

Gsus2      E♭maj7♯11      Gsus2

No one mourns the wick - ed When at last they're

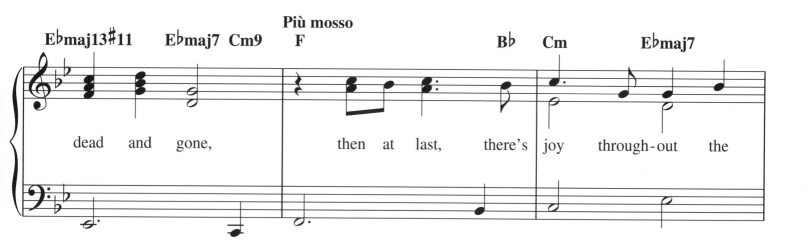

E♭maj13♯11   E♭maj7 Cm9   **Più mosso** F      B♭   Cm    E♭maj7

dead and gone, then at last, there's joy through-out the

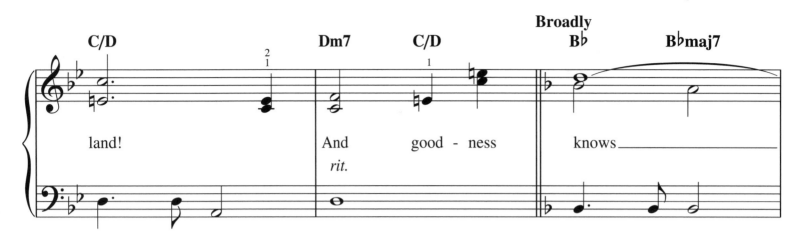

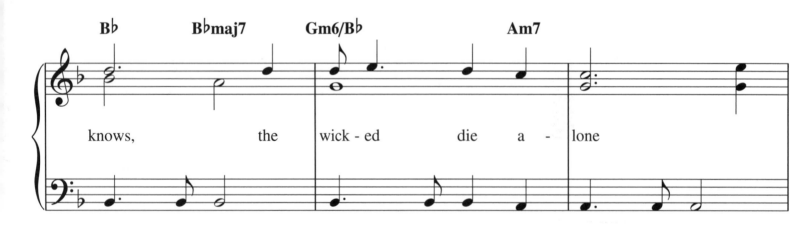

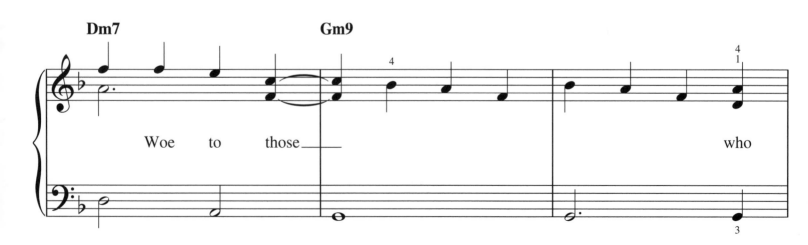

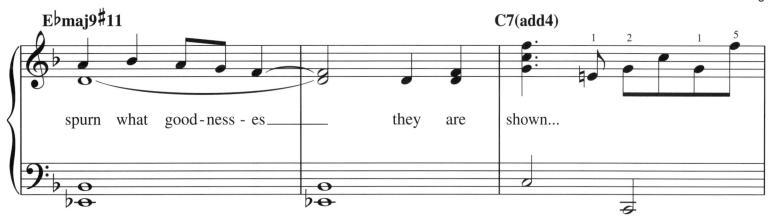

spurn what good-ness-es_____ they are shown...

cresc.

No one mourns the wick-ed!

No one mourns the wick-ed!

**Dm**

**Bb/D**

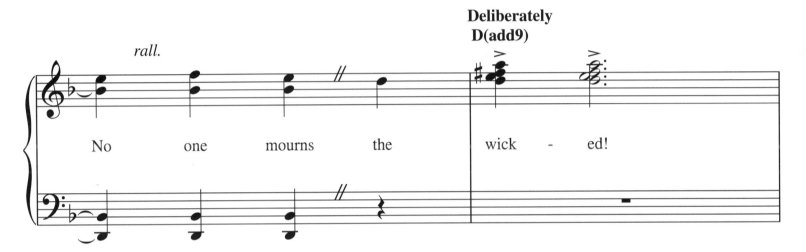

**Deliberately**
**D(add9)**

*rall.*

No one mourns the wick - ed!

**N.C.**

Wick - ed!

*8vb*

*8vb*

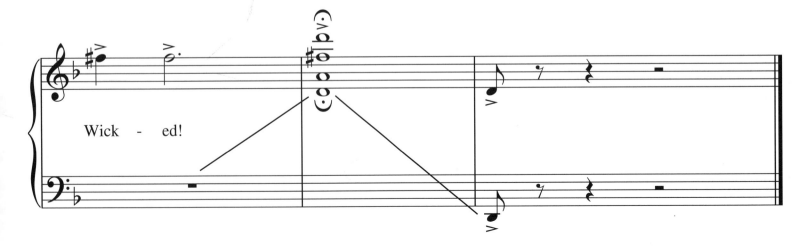

Wick - ed!

# THE WIZARD AND I

Music and Lyrics by
STEPHEN SCHWARTZ

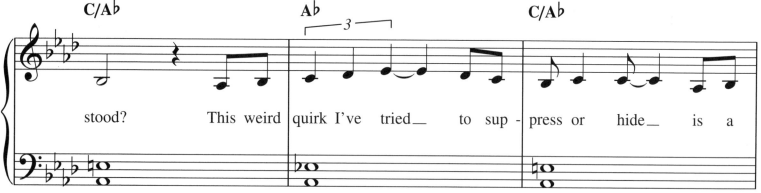

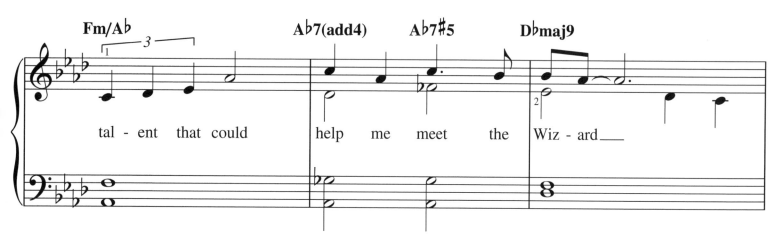

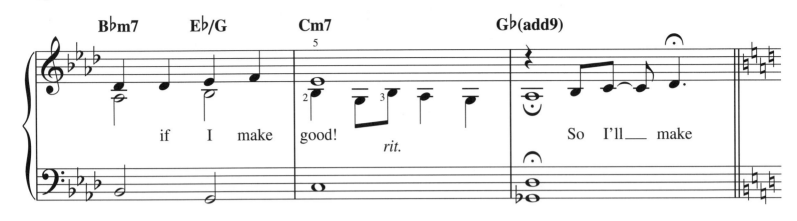

if I make good! *rit.* So I'll___ make

**Pulsing with excitement**

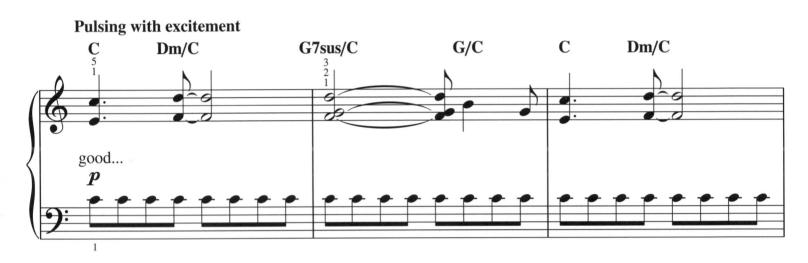

good...
*p*

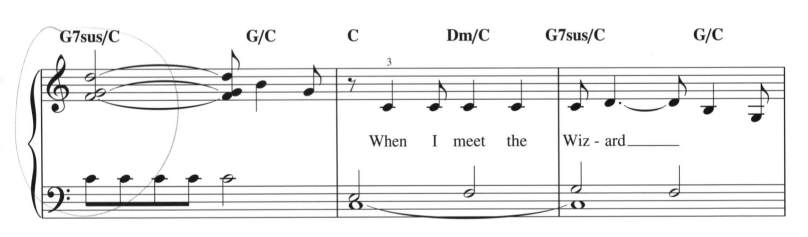

When I meet the Wiz - ard___

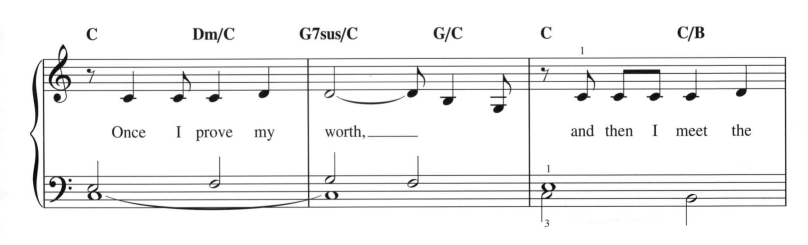

Once I prove my worth,___ and then I meet the

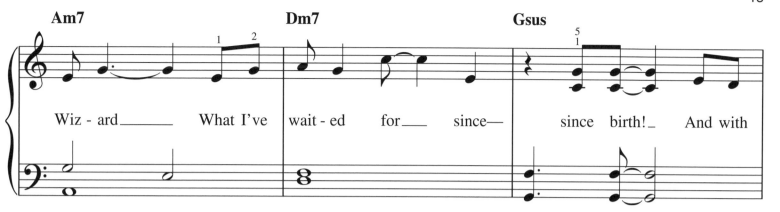

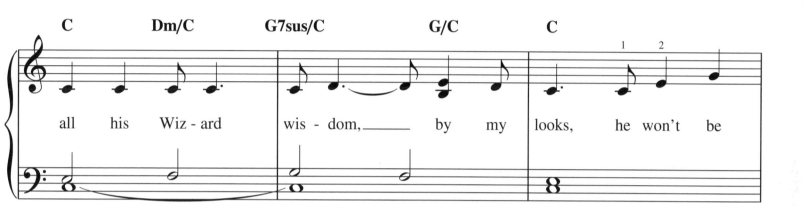

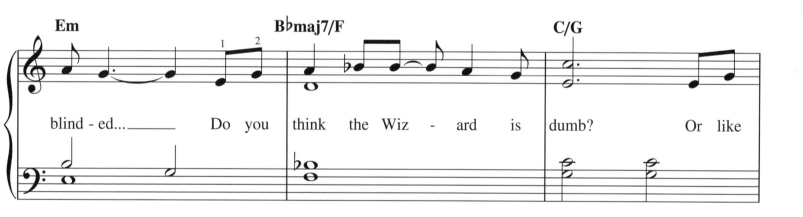

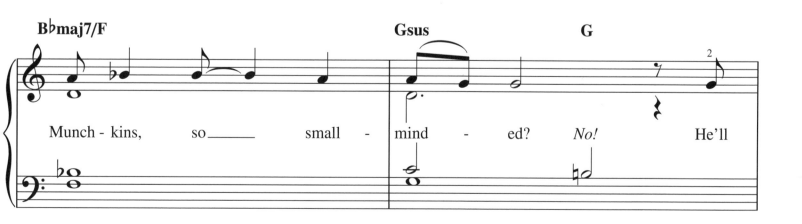

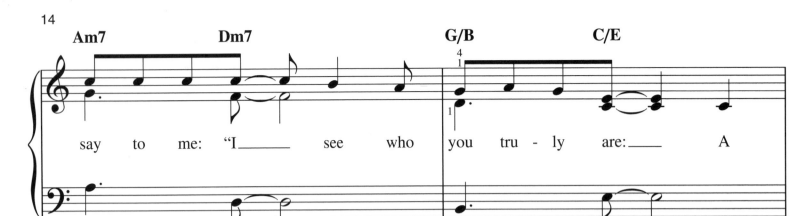

say to me: "I_____ see who you tru - ly are:_____ A

girl on whom I_____ can re - ly!" And that's how we'll_ be -

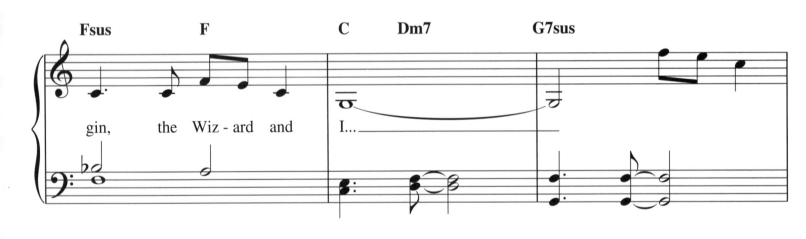

gin, the Wiz - ard and I..._____

Once I'm with the

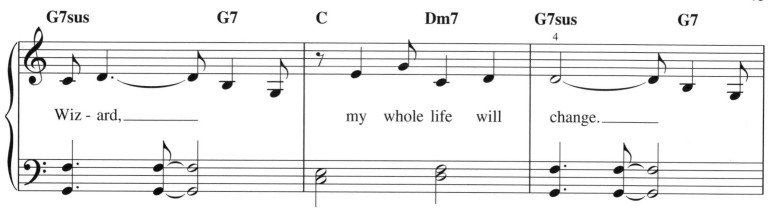

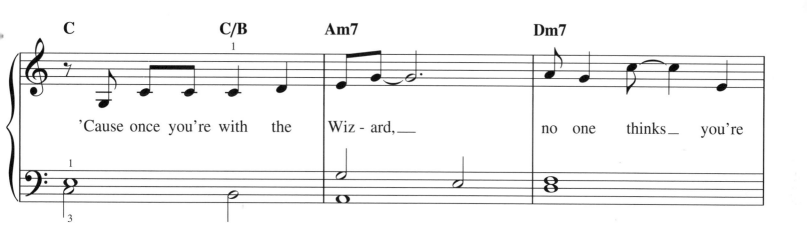

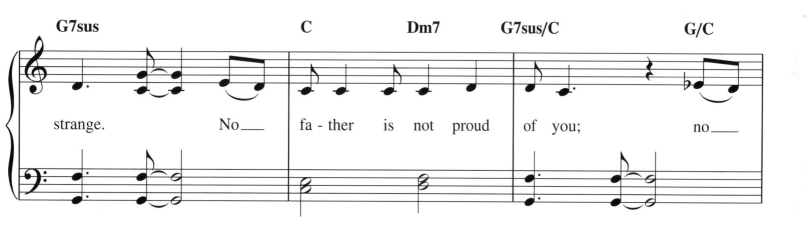

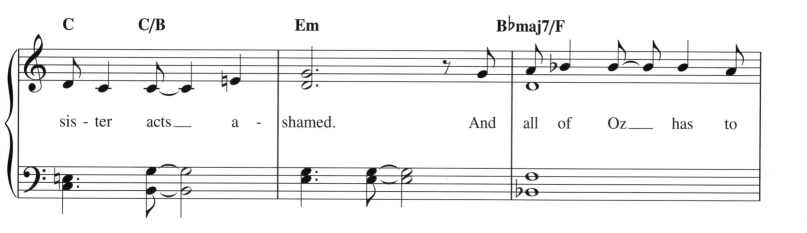

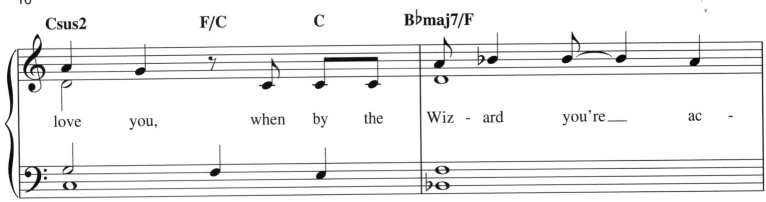

**Csus2**    **F/C**    **C**    **B♭maj7/F**

love you,    when by the    Wiz - ard    you're___    ac -

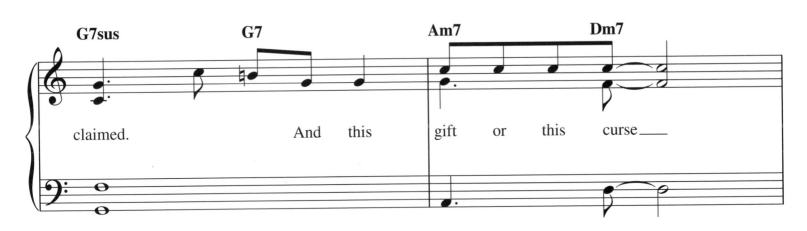

**G7sus**    **G7**    **Am7**    **Dm7**

claimed.    And this    gift    or    this    curse___

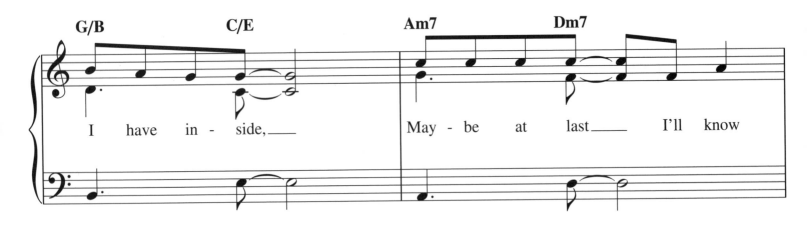

**G/B**    **C/E**    **Am7**    **Dm7**

I    have    in - side,___    May - be    at    last___    I'll    know

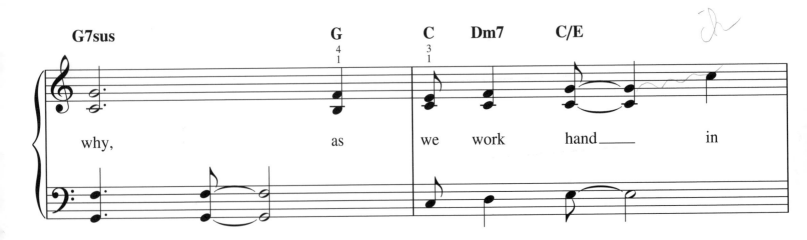

**G7sus**    **G**    **C**    **Dm7**    **C/E**

why,    as    we    work    hand___    in

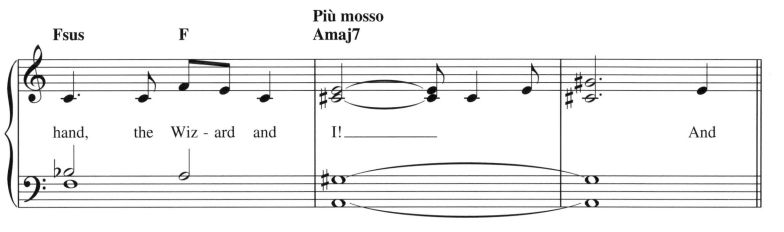

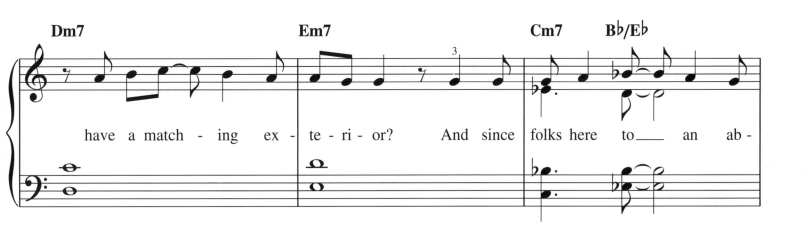

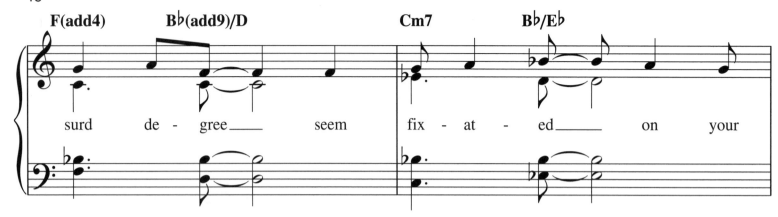

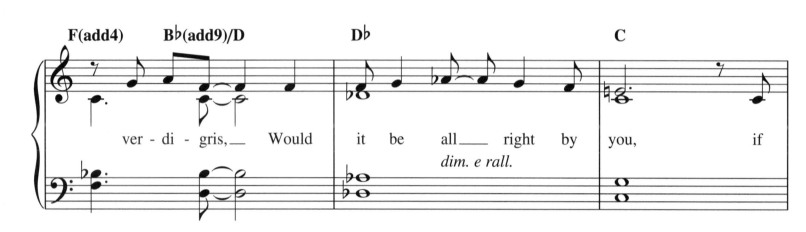

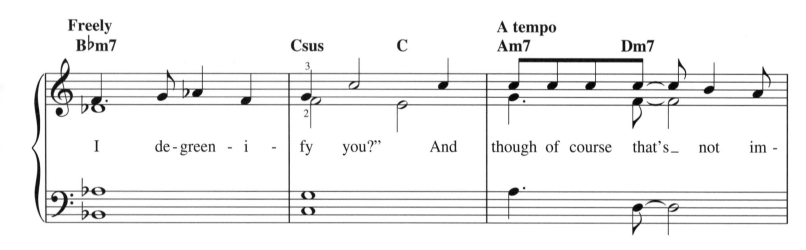

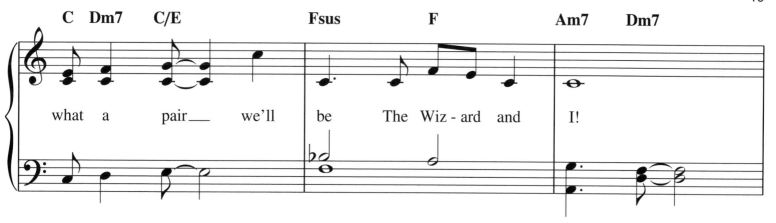

what a pair___ we'll be  The Wiz - ard  and  I!

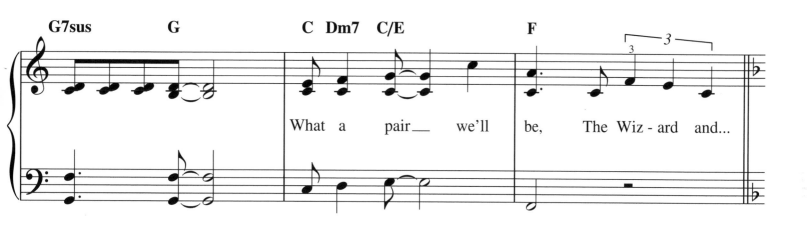

What a  pair___ we'll be,  The Wiz - ard  and...

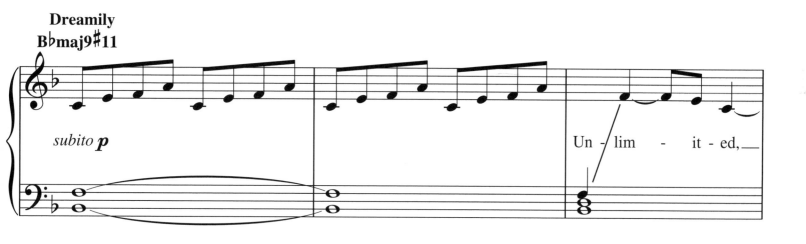

subito **p**

Un - lim - it - ed,___

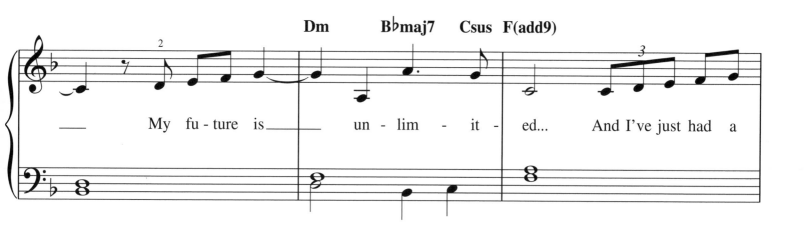

___  My fu - ture is___  un - lim - it - ed...  And I've just had a

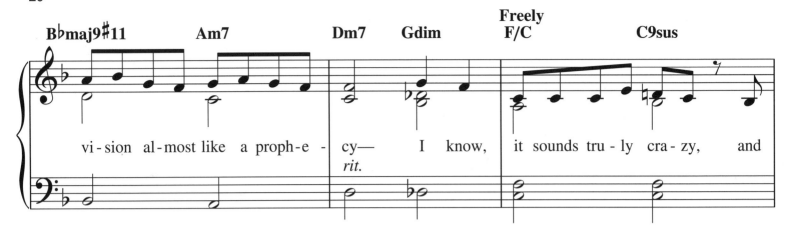

vi-sion al-most like a proph-e - cy— I know, it sounds tru-ly cra - zy, and

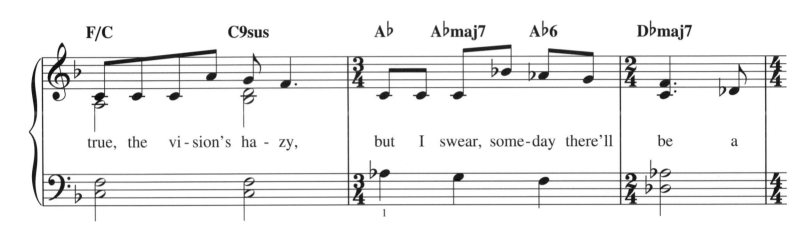

true, the vi-sion's ha - zy, but I swear, some-day there'll be a

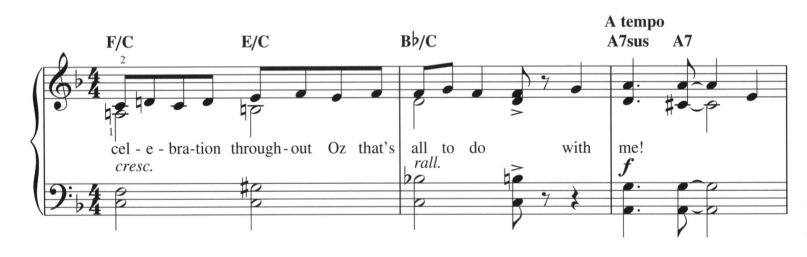

cel - e - bra-tion through-out Oz that's all to do with me!

And I'll

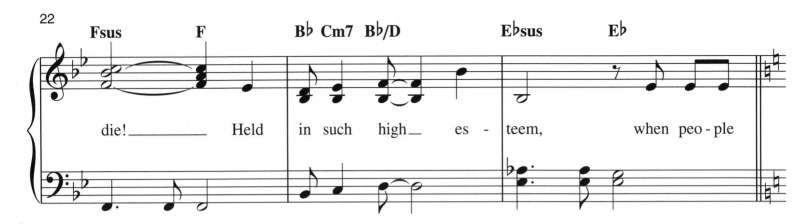

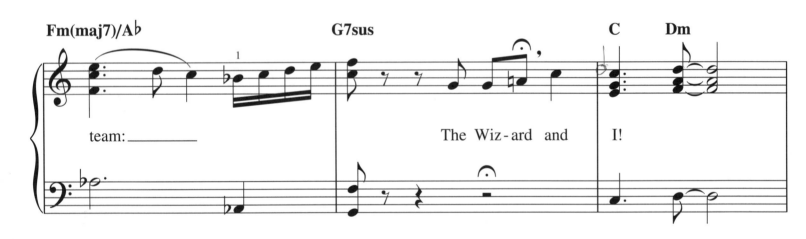

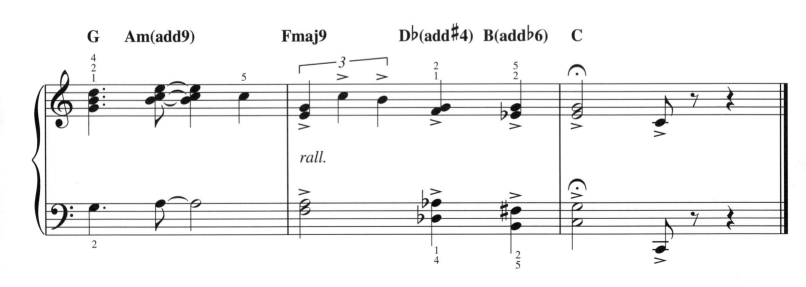

# WHAT IS THIS FEELING?

Music and Lyrics by
STEPHEN SCHWARTZ

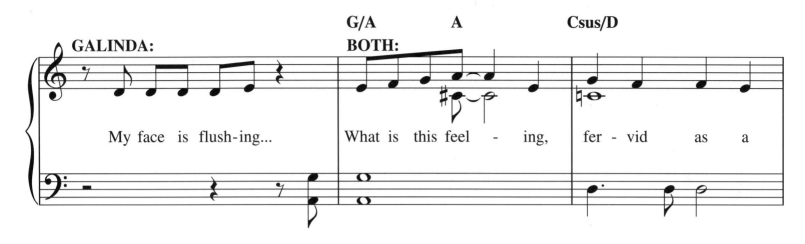

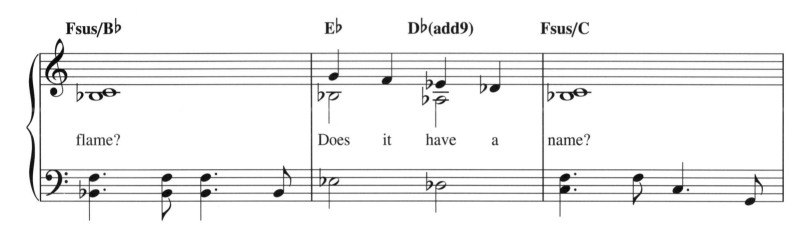

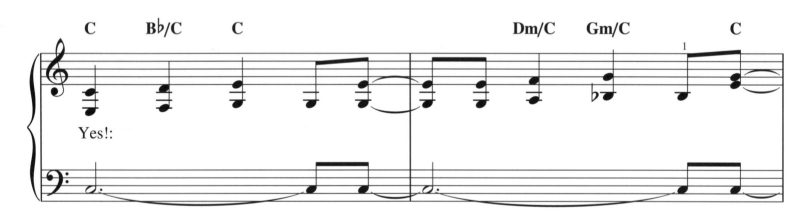

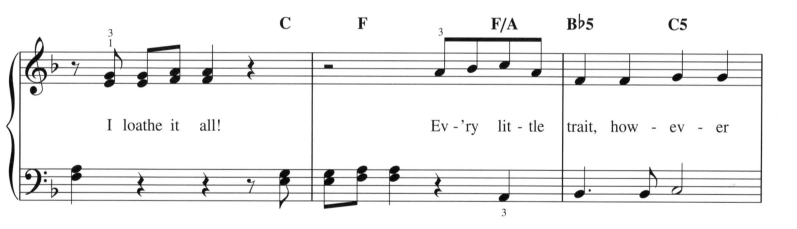

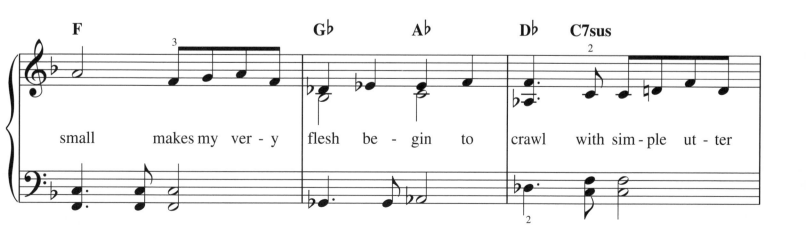

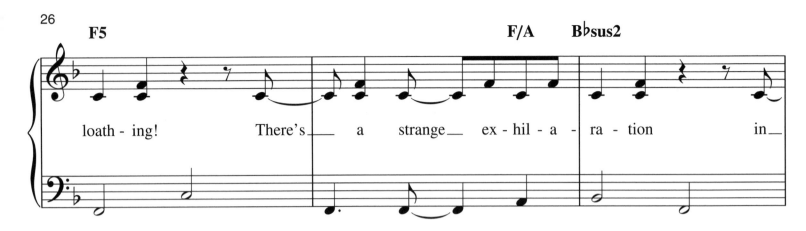

loath - ing! There's a strange ex - hil - a - ra - tion in

_____ such to - tal de - tes - ta - tion It's so pure!_ So

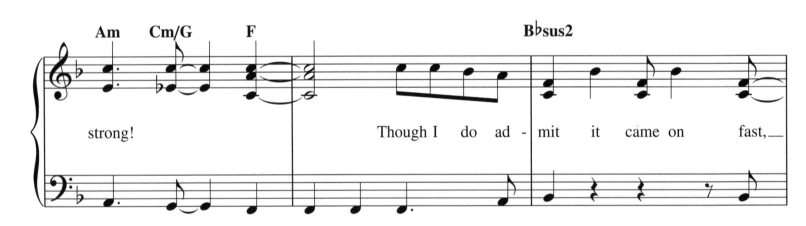

strong! Though I do ad - mit it came on fast,_

_____ still I do be - lieve that it_____ can last, And I will be

loath - ing,__ loath - ing you my whole

life... What is this feel-ing, so sud-den and new?__

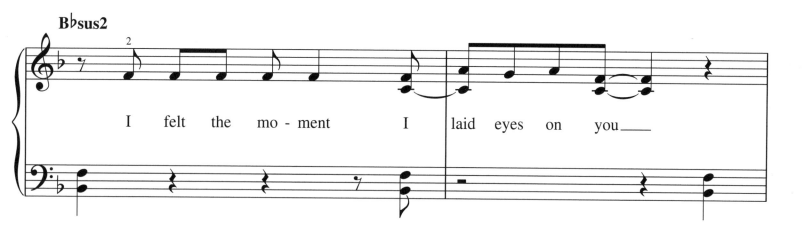

I felt the mo - ment I laid eyes on you____

My pulse is rush - ing, My head is reel - ing,

ra - tion    in____ such to - tal de - tes - ta - tion

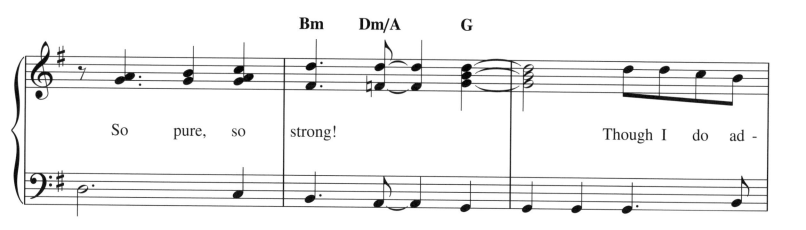

So    pure,  so    strong!                    Though I   do   ad -

mit  it  came on    fast,____      still I  do  be - lieve  that it____   can

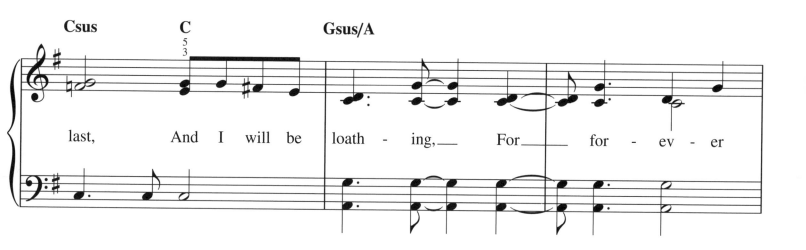

last,       And  I  will be    loath - ing,____  For____   for - ev - er

loath - ing, _____ Tru - ly, deep - ly

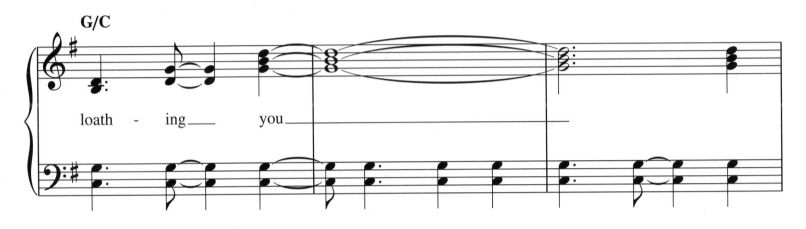

loath - ing _____ you _____

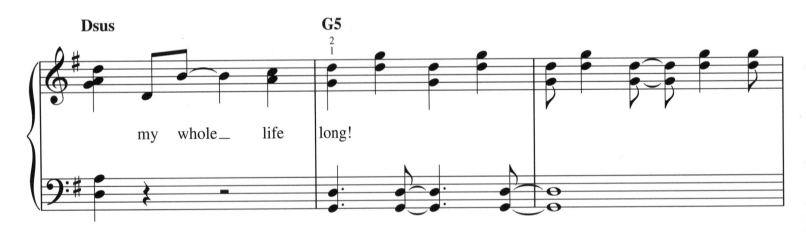

my whole_ life long!

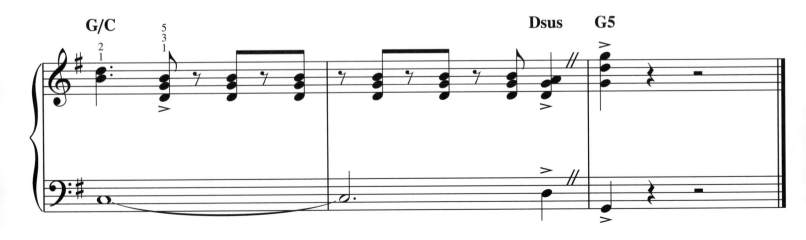

# DANCING THROUGH LIFE

Music and Lyrics by
STEPHEN SCHWARTZ

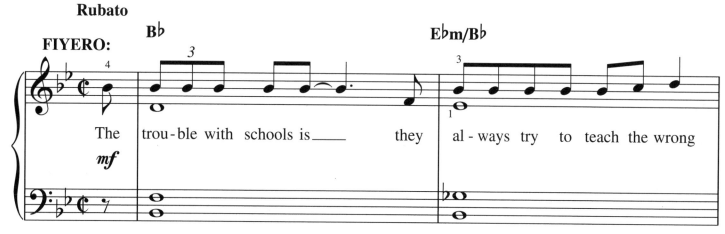

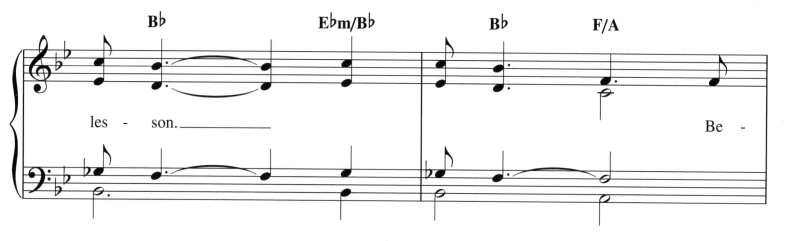

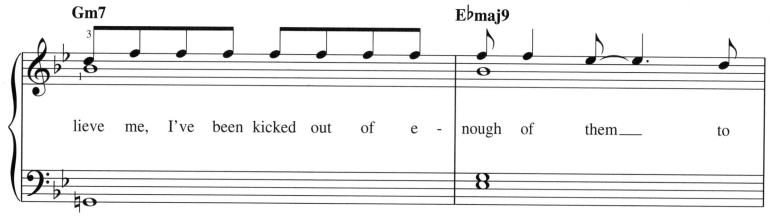

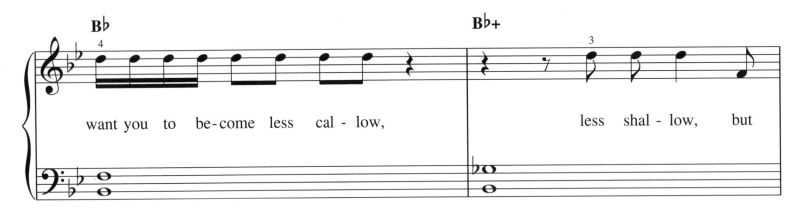

want you to be-come less cal - low,          less shal - low, but

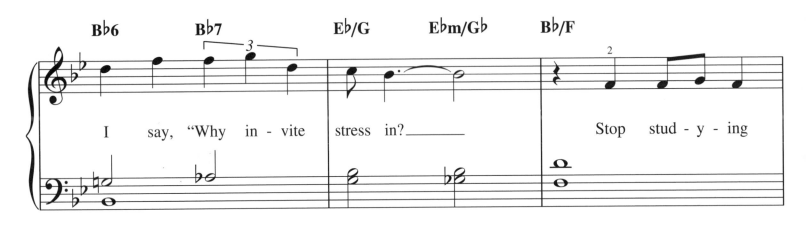

I    say, "Why in - vite   stress in?_____          Stop   stud - y - ing

strife          and   learn to live 'the un - ex - am-ined   life' "...

*mp legato*

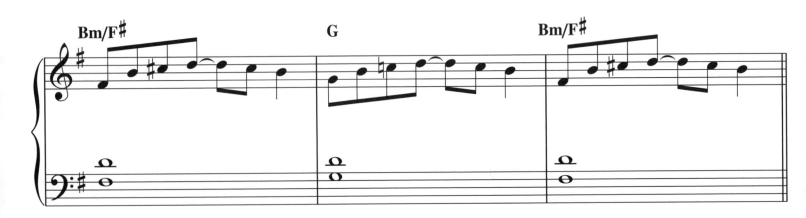

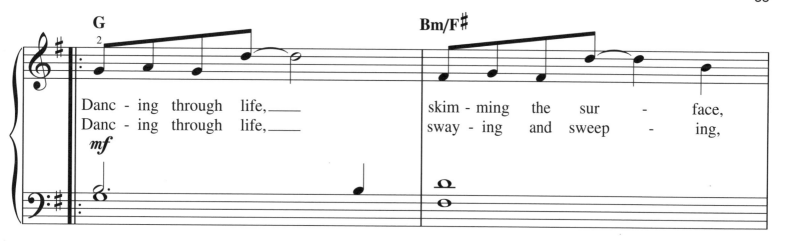

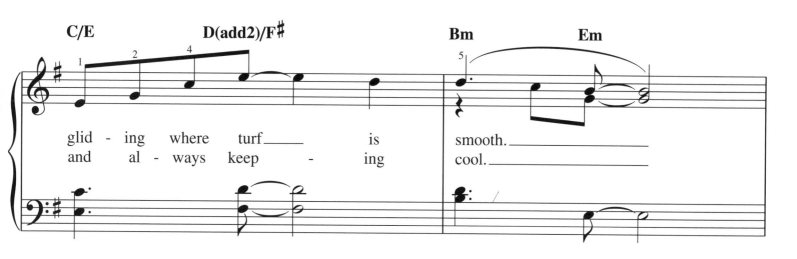

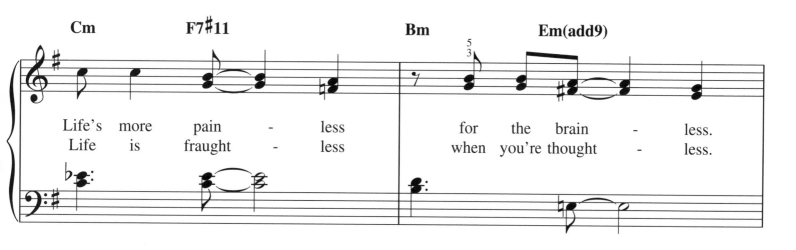

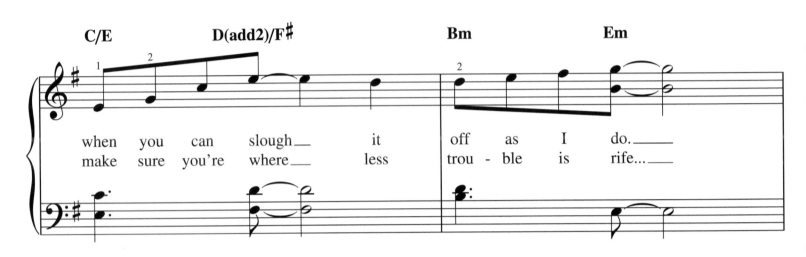

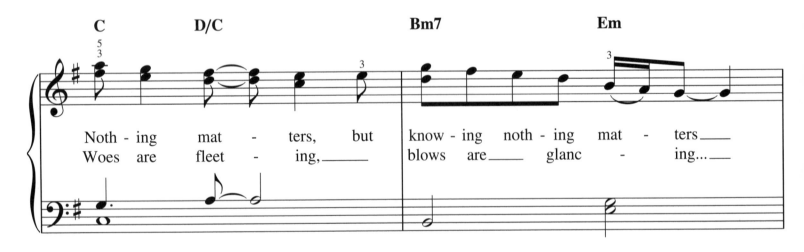

light._____ Find the pret - ti - est girl..._ Give 'er a whirl_____

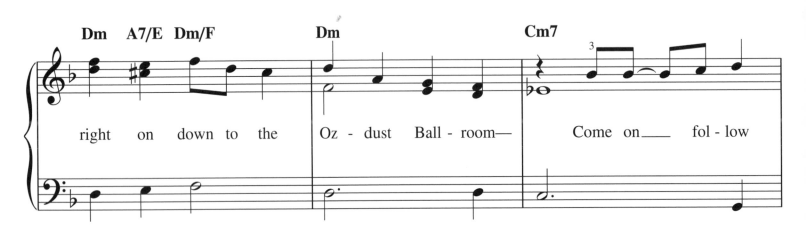

right on down to the Oz - dust Ball - room— Come on___ fol - low

me,___ you'll be hap - py to be there..._

*cresc.*

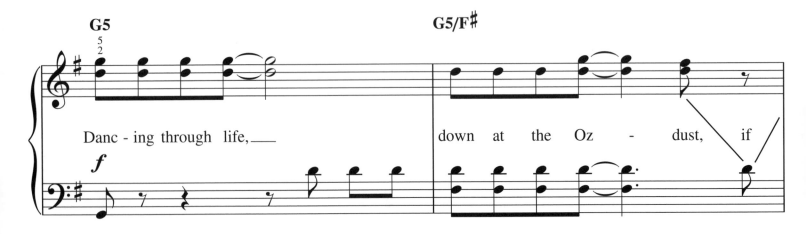

Danc - ing through life,___ down at the Oz - dust, if

*f*

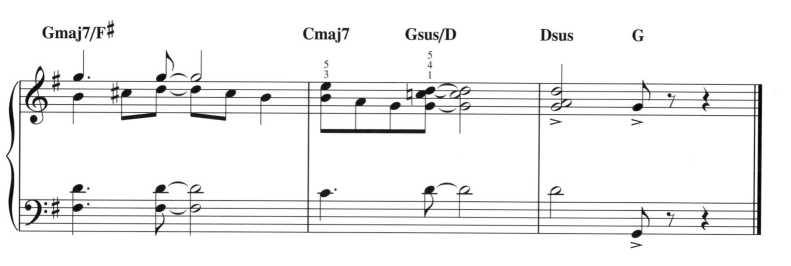

# POPULAR

Music and Lyrics by
STEPHEN SCHWARTZ

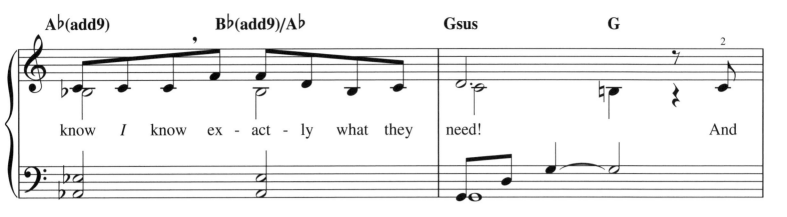

know *I* know ex - act - ly what they need! And

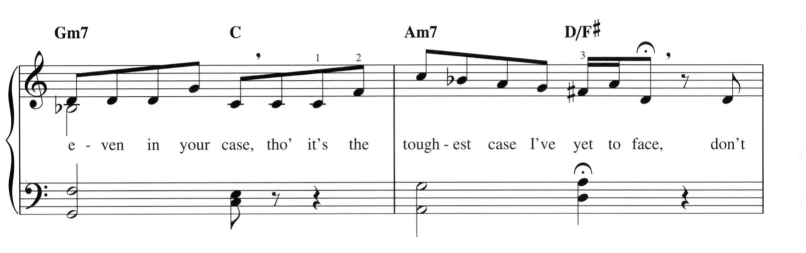

e - ven in your case, tho' it's the tough - est case I've yet to face, don't

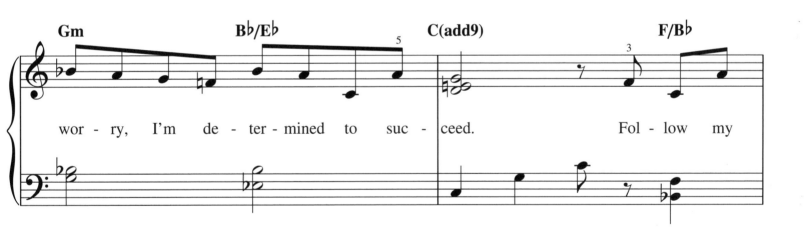

wor - ry, I'm de - ter - mined to suc - ceed. Fol - low my

lead and yes, in - deed you will be...

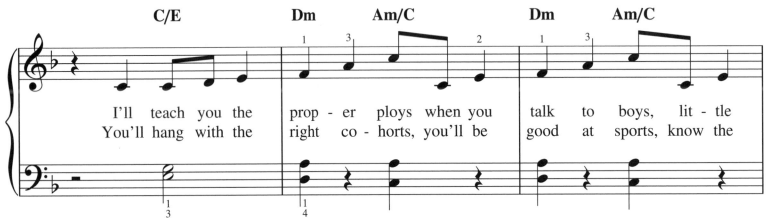

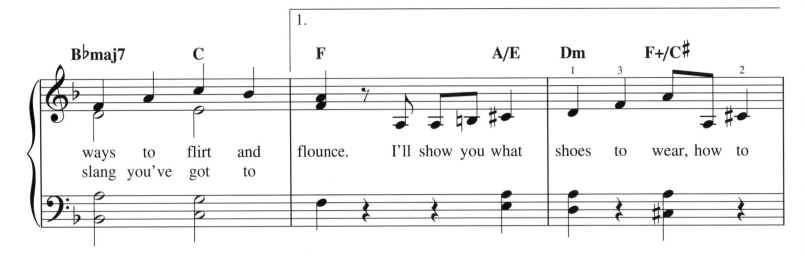

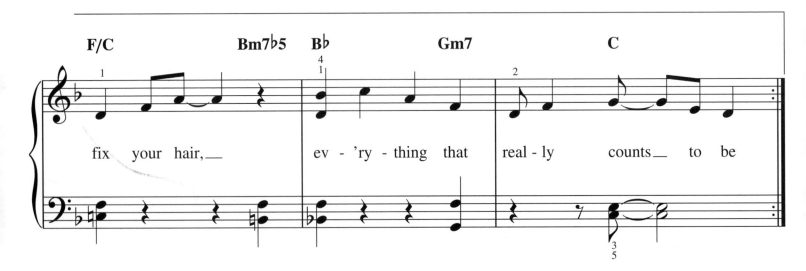

**2.**

A7sus    D        Gm7                          C

know        So let's    start,  'cause you've got  an   aw-f'lly long way  to

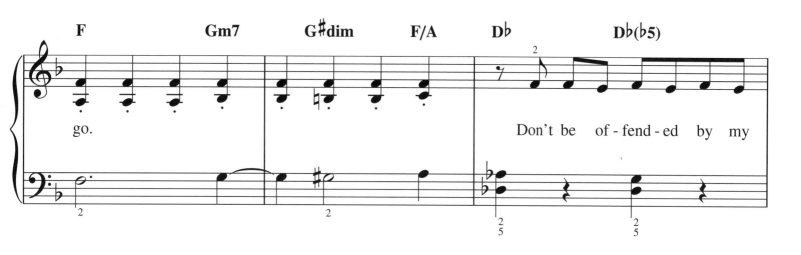

F        Gm7     G#dim   F/A    Db      Db(b5)

go.                            Don't be of-fend-ed by my

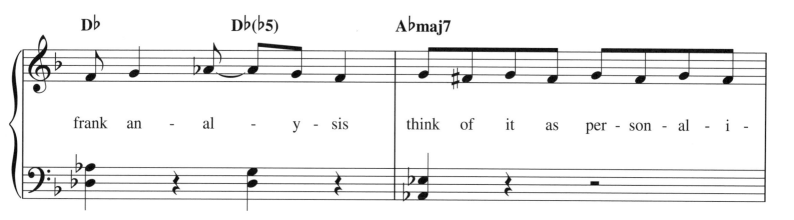

Db       Db(b5)     Abmaj7

frank an - al - y - sis    think of it as per-son-al-i-

Ab/Eb   Dbm7         Dbm6

ty di - al - y - sis.    Now that I've chos-en to be-

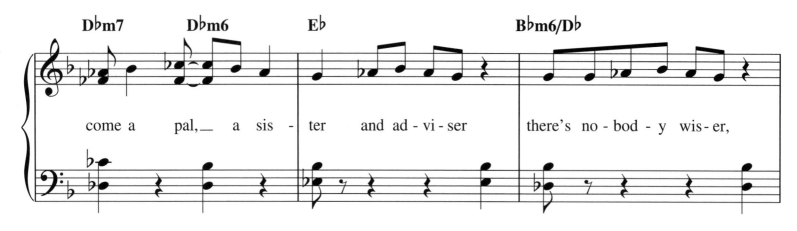

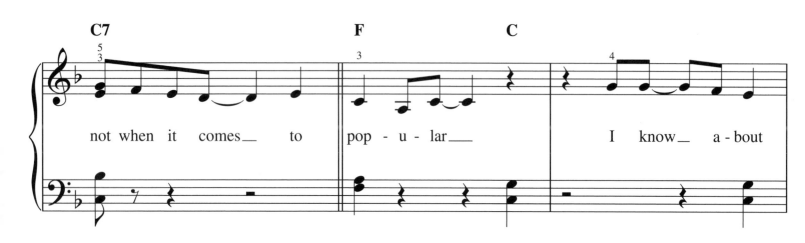

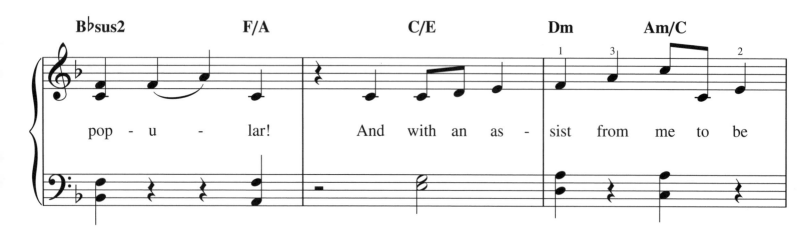

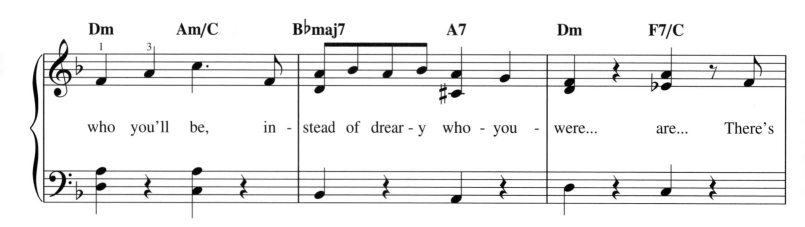

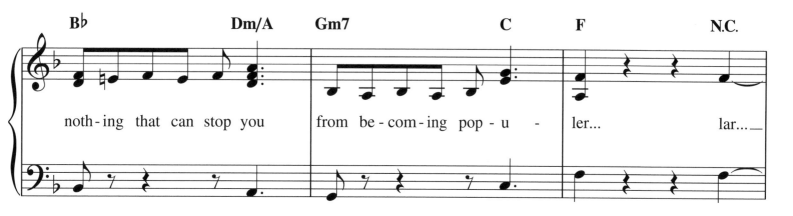

noth-ing that can stop you from be - com-ing pop - u - ler... lar...

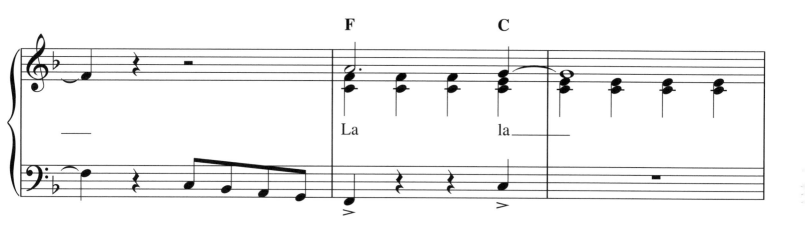

La la

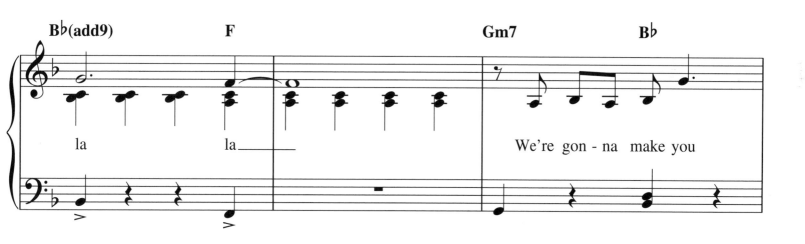

la la We're gon - na make you

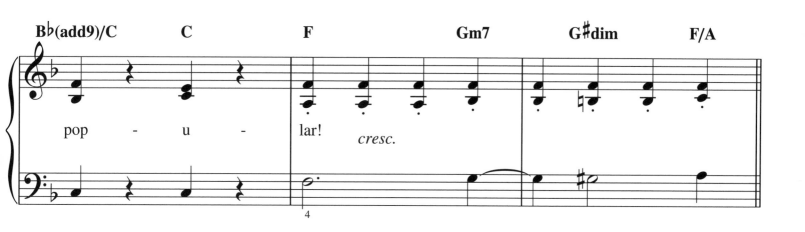

pop - u - lar! *cresc.*

44

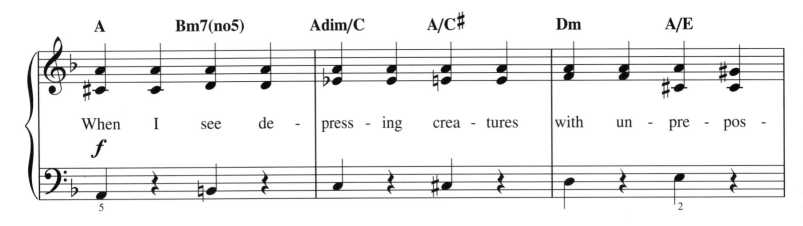

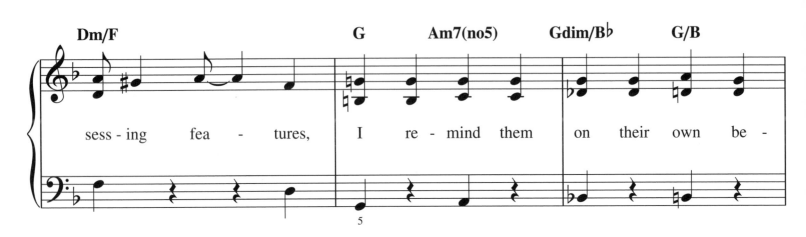

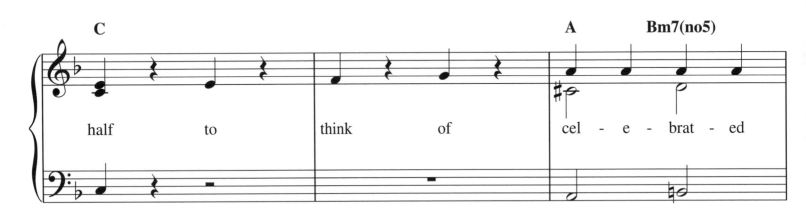

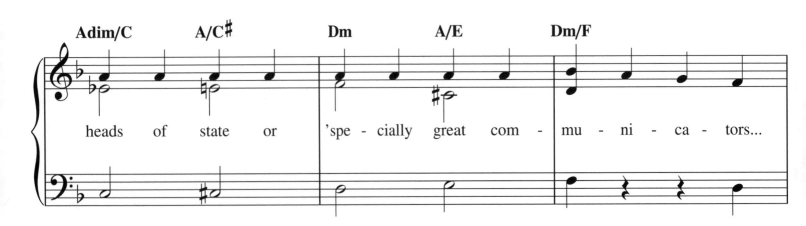

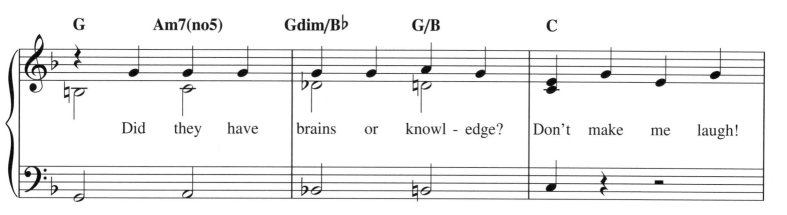

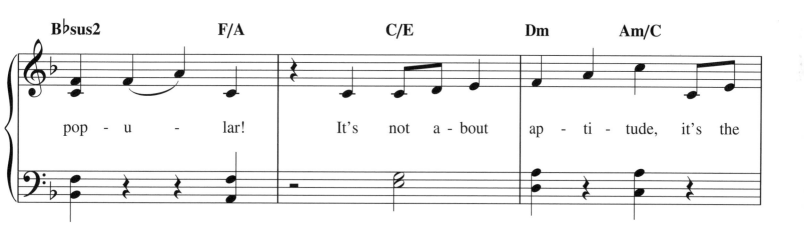

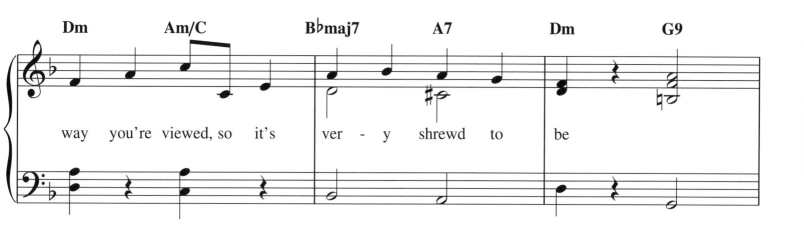

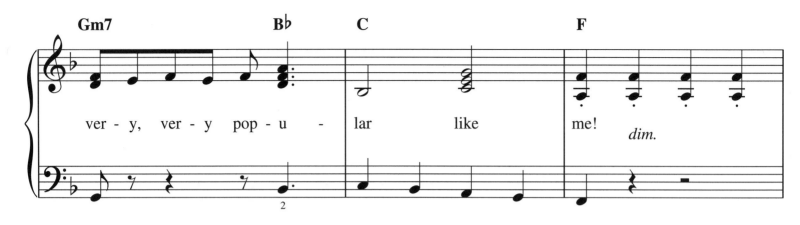

ver - y, ver - y pop - u - lar　　like　　me!

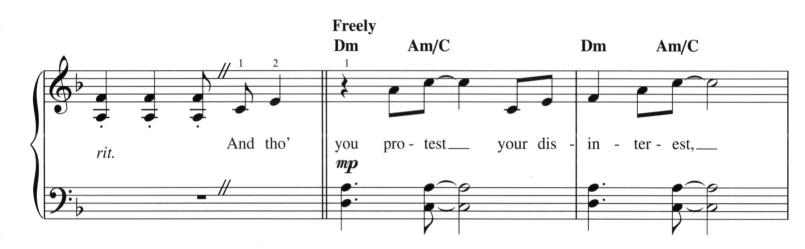

**Freely**

And tho' you pro - test___ your dis - in - ter - est,___

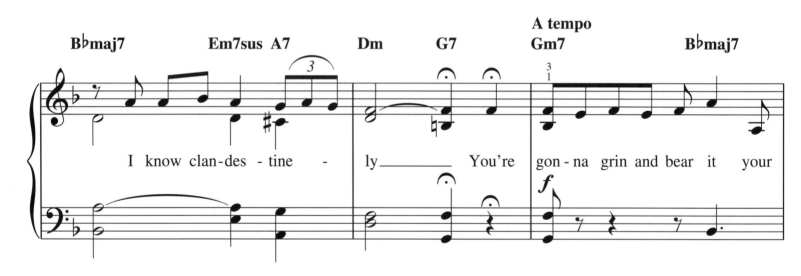

**A tempo**

I know clan-des - tine - ly_____ You're gon - na grin and bear it your

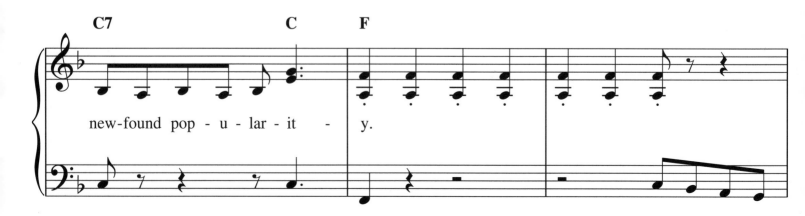

new-found pop - u - lar - it - y.

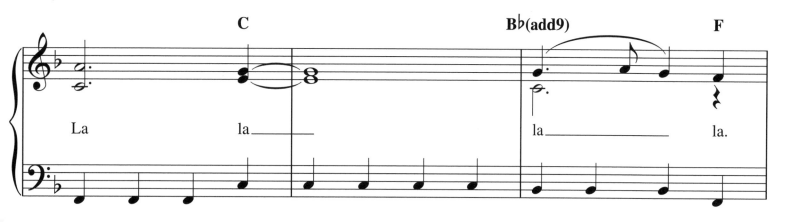

La          la          la          la.

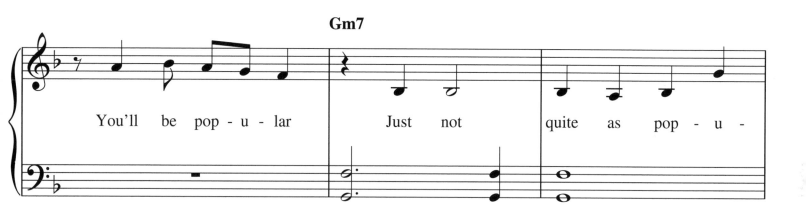

You'll    be    pop - u - lar          Just    not          quite    as    pop - u -

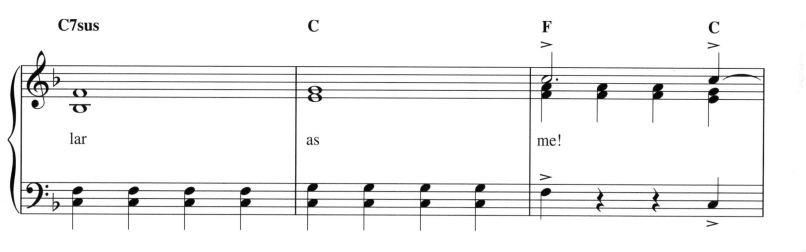

lar          as          me!

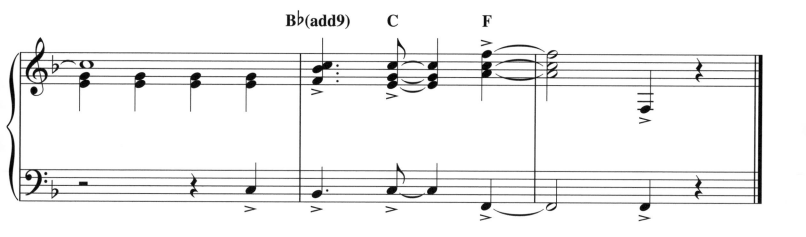

# I'M NOT THAT GIRL

Music and Lyrics by
STEPHEN SCHWARTZ

**Sweet and steady, like a music box**

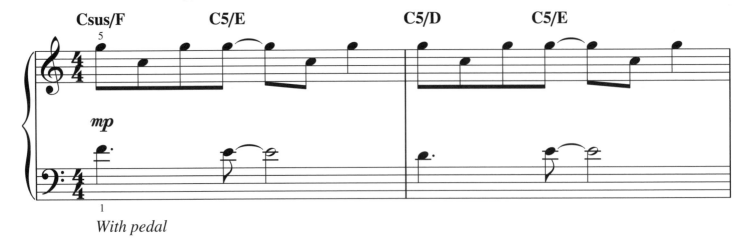

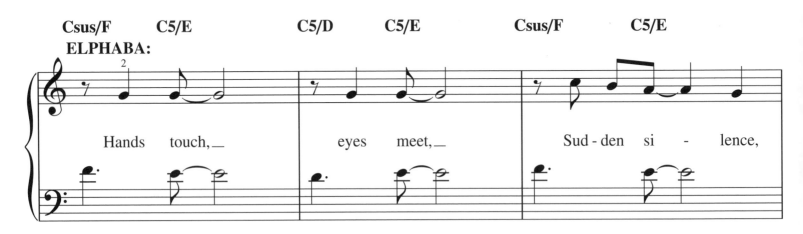

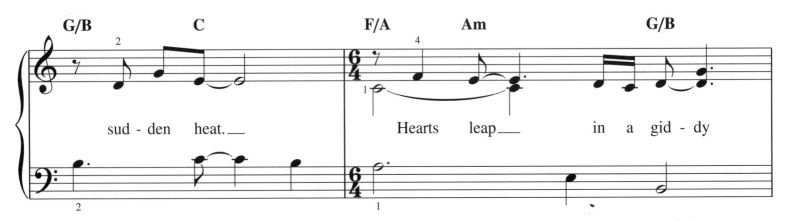

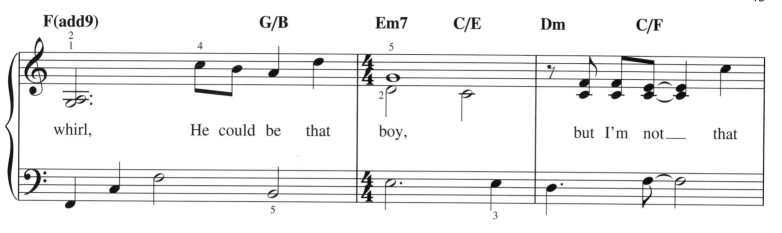

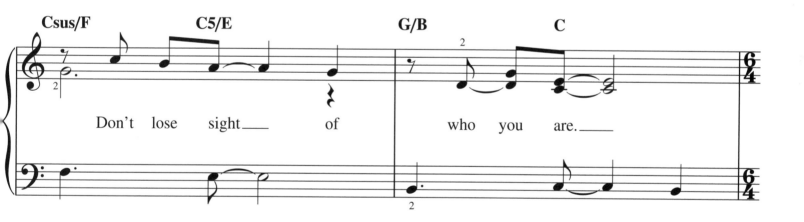

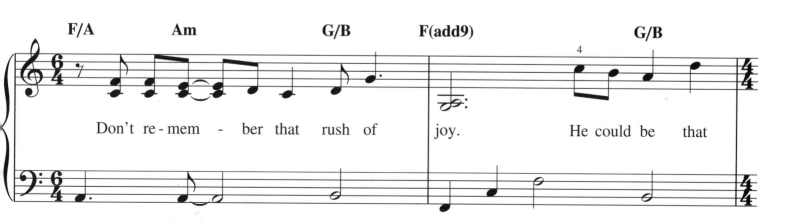

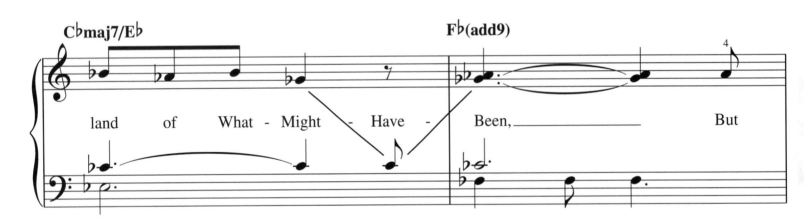

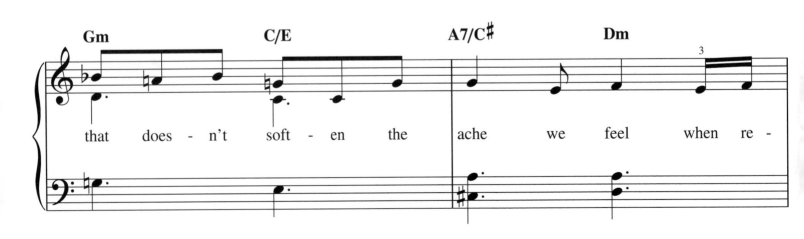

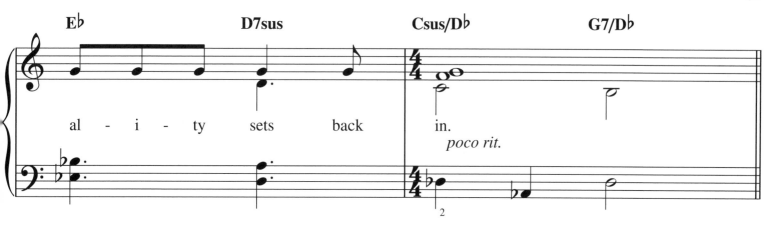

al - i - ty sets back in. *poco rit.*

A Tempo

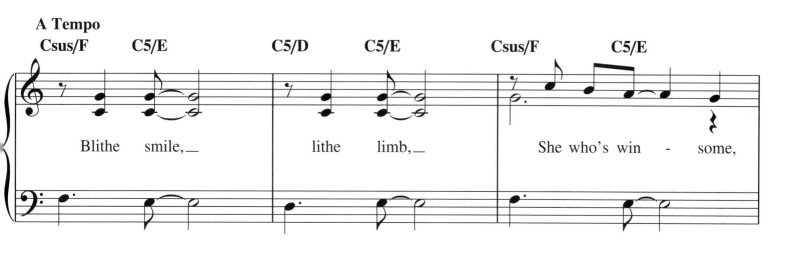

Blithe smile,— lithe limb,— She who's win - some,

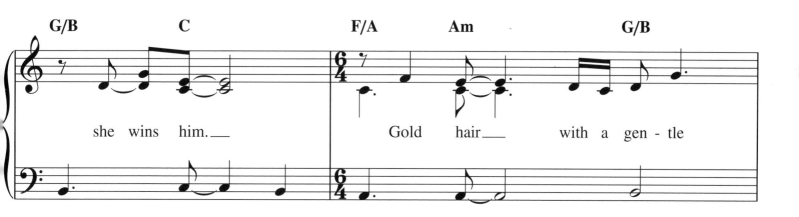

she wins him.— Gold hair— with a gen - tle

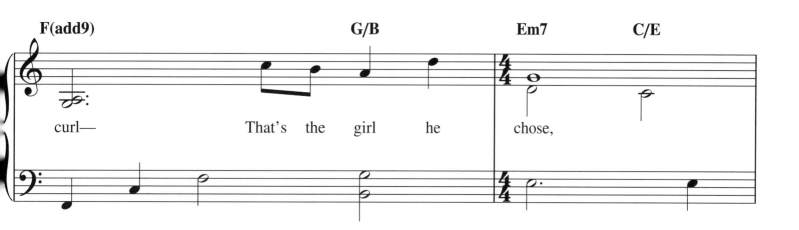

curl— That's the girl he chose,

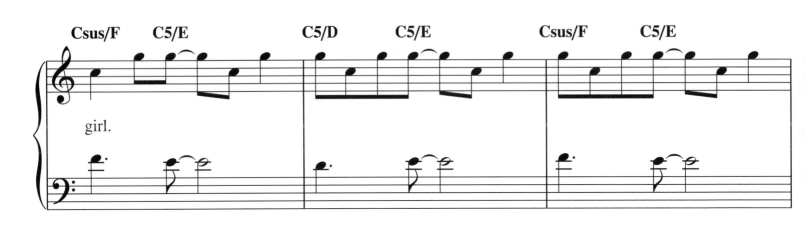

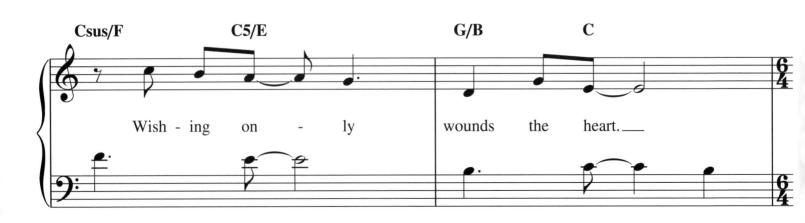

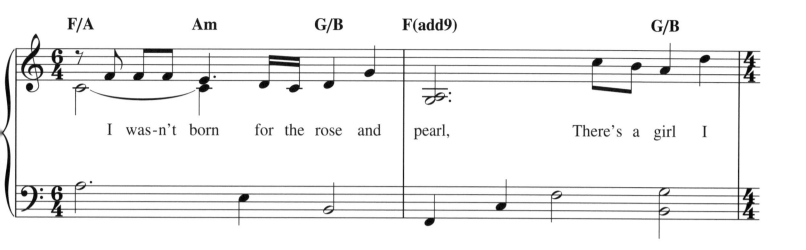

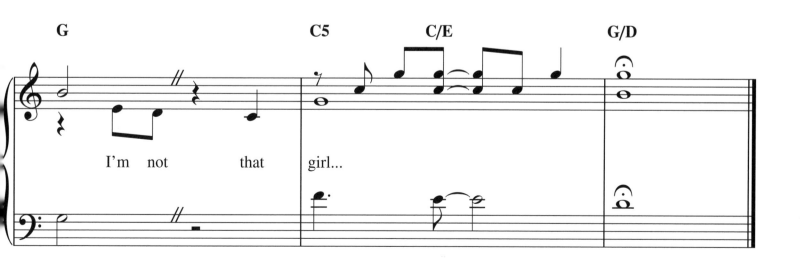

# ONE SHORT DAY

Music and Lyrics by
STEPHEN SCHWARTZ

Em - er-ald Cit - y, One short day__ full of so much to do,__

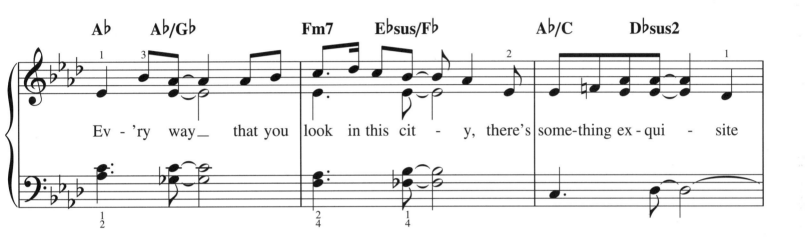

Ev - 'ry way__ that you look in this cit - y, there's some-thing ex - qui - site

you'll want to vis - it be - fore the day's through!__

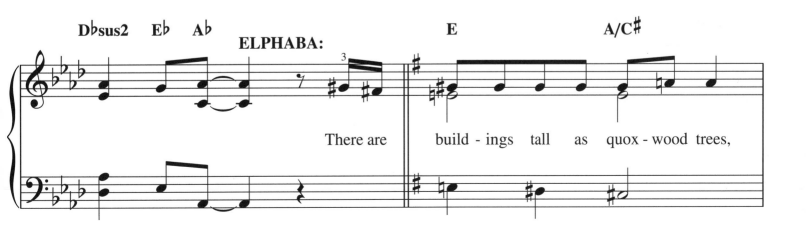

**ELPHABA:**

There are build - ings tall as quox - wood trees,

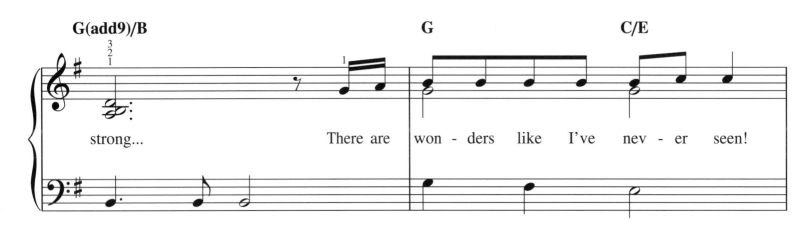

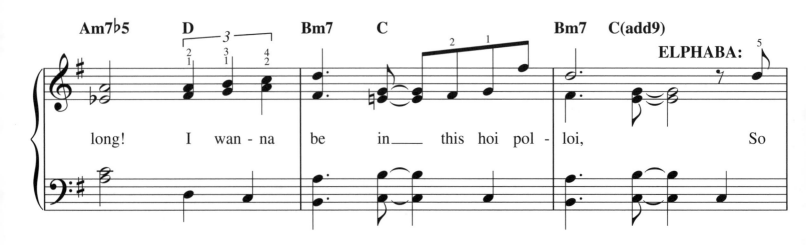

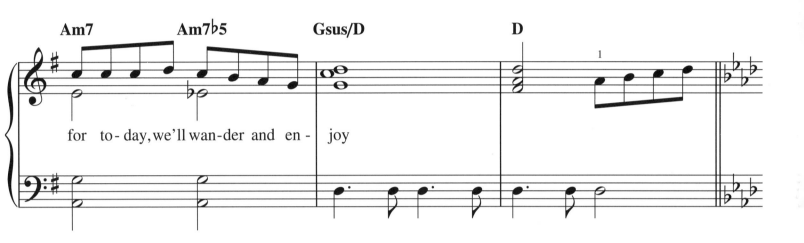

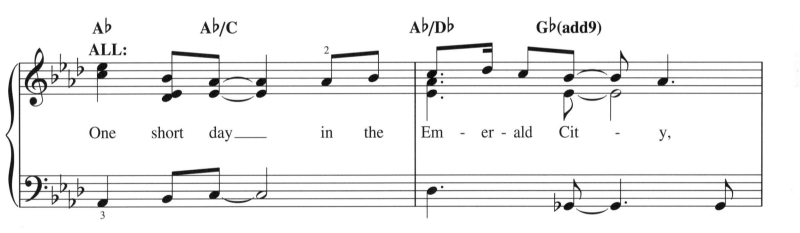

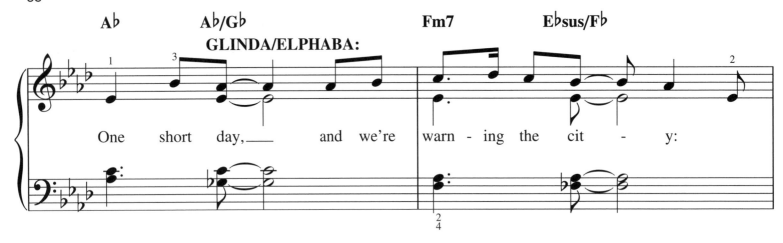

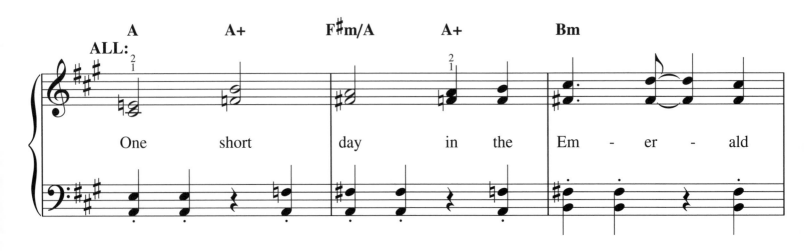

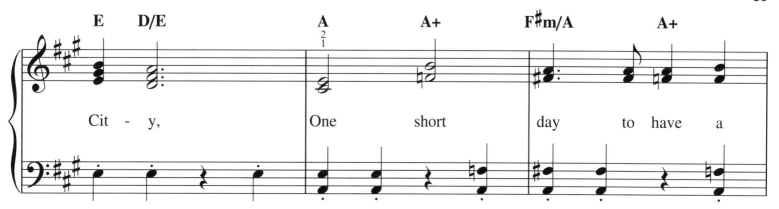
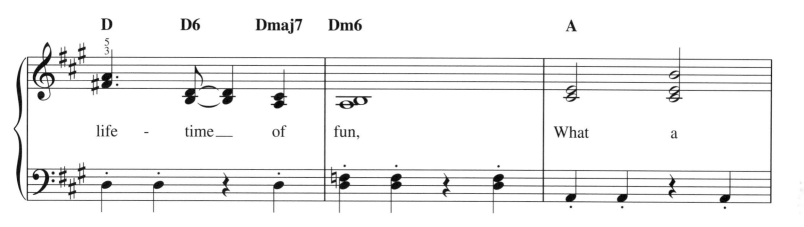
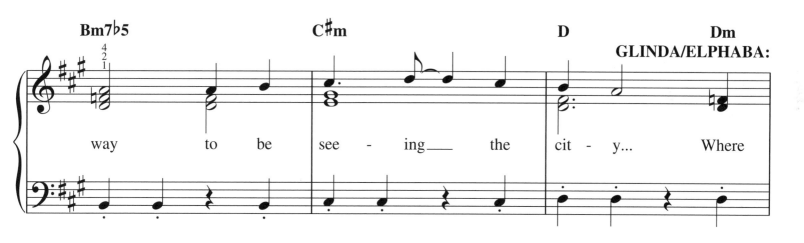

And then, just like now, we can say: We're

**Slower**

ELPHABA:

GLINDA:

just two friends... Two good friends... Two *best* friends...

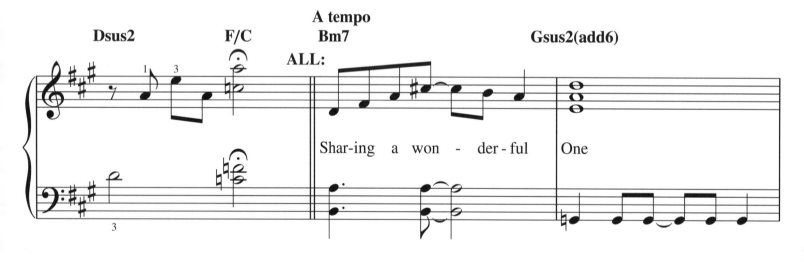

**A tempo**

ALL:

Shar-ing a won - der - ful One

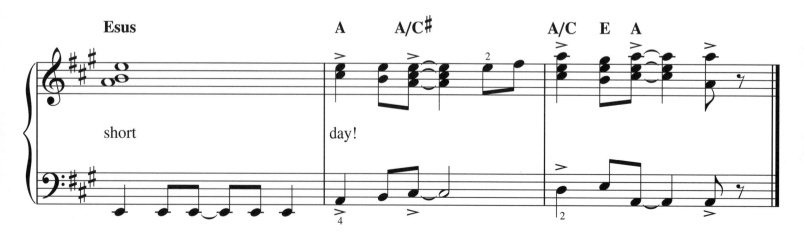

short day!

# DEFYING GRAVITY

Music and Lyrics by
STEPHEN SCHWARTZ

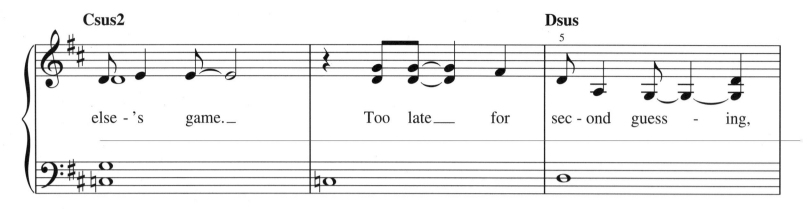

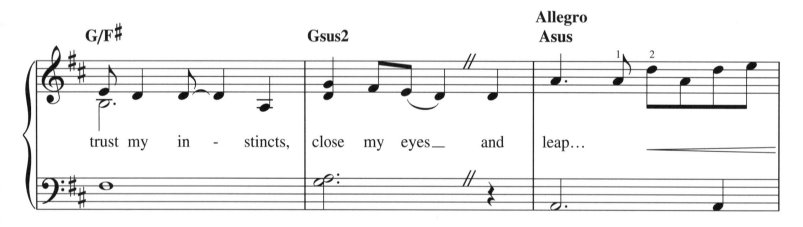

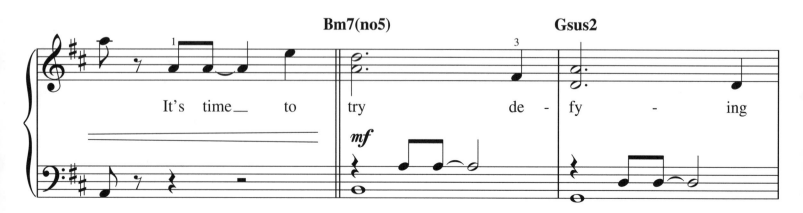

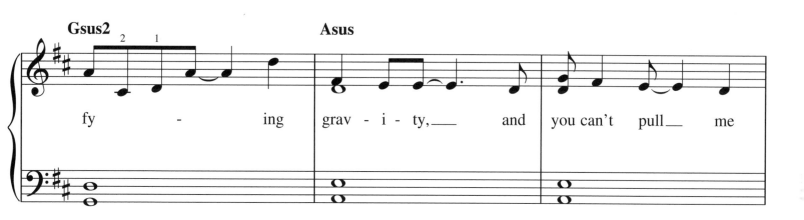

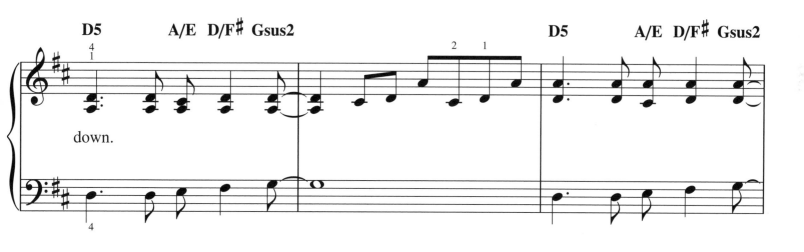

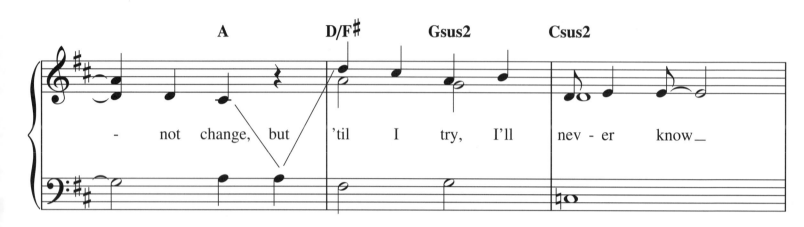

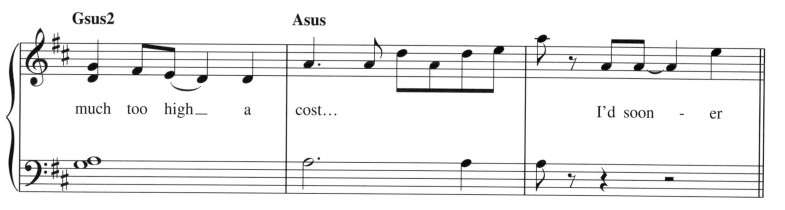

much too high\_ a cost... I'd soon - er

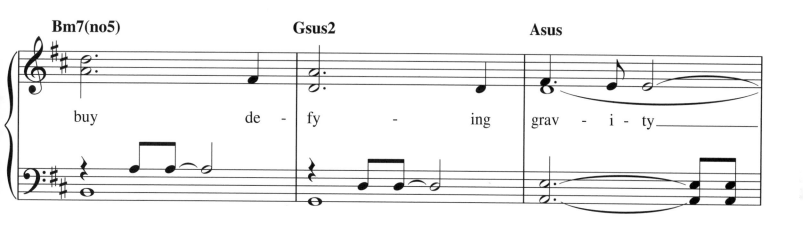

buy de - fy - ing grav - i - ty\_

\_ Kiss me\_ good - bye,\_ I'm de - fy - ing

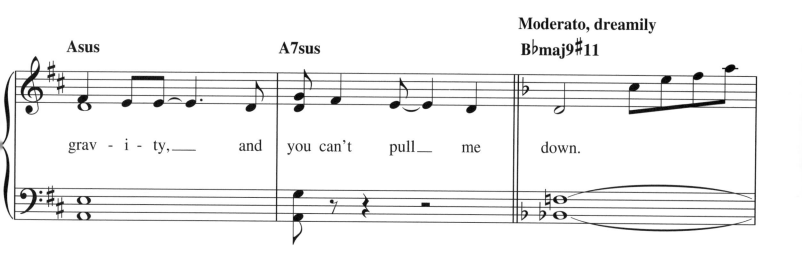

grav - i - ty,\_ and you can't pull\_ me down.

dim.

*p*

Un - lim - it - ed... My fu-ture is

**C**

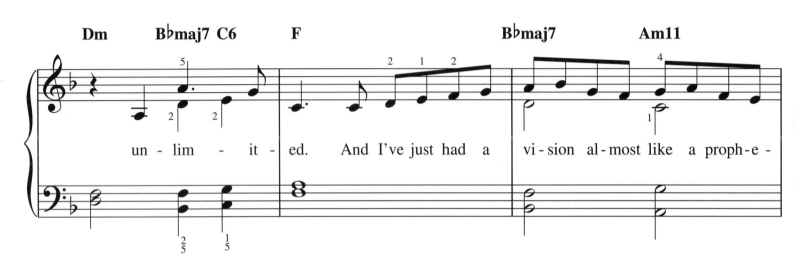

**Dm**  **B♭maj7 C6**  **F**  **B♭maj7**  **Am11**

un - lim - it - ed. And I've just had a vi - sion al-most like a proph-e -

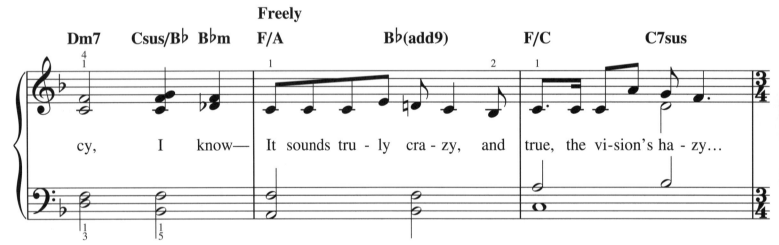

**Dm7**  **Csus/B♭ B♭m**  **F/A**  **B♭(add9)**  **F/C**  **C7sus**

Freely

cy, I know— It sounds tru-ly cra-zy, and true, the vi-sion's ha-zy...

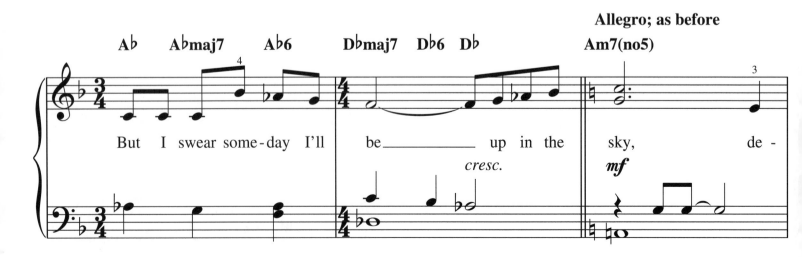

**A♭**  **A♭maj7**  **A♭6**  **D♭maj7  D♭6  D♭**

Allegro; as before

**Am7(no5)**

But I swear some-day I'll be_____ up in the sky, de -

*cresc.*

*mf*

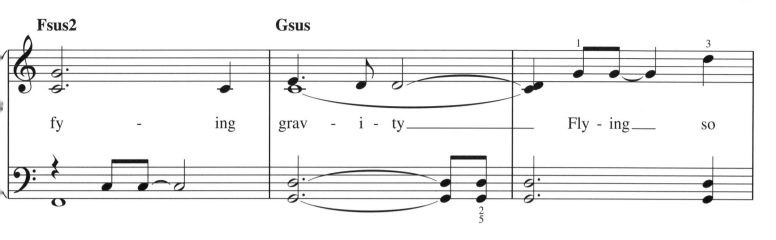

Fsus2　　　　　　　Gsus

fy - ing grav - i - ty_____ Fly - ing__ so

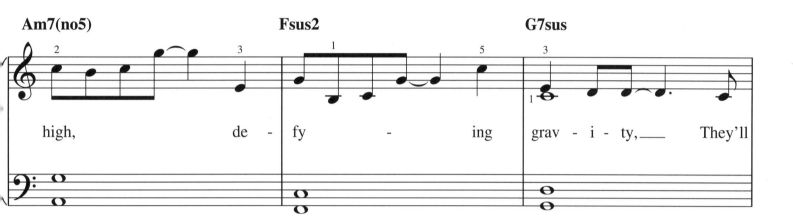

Am7(no5)　　　　　Fsus2　　　　　G7sus

high, de - fy - ing grav - i - ty,__ They'll

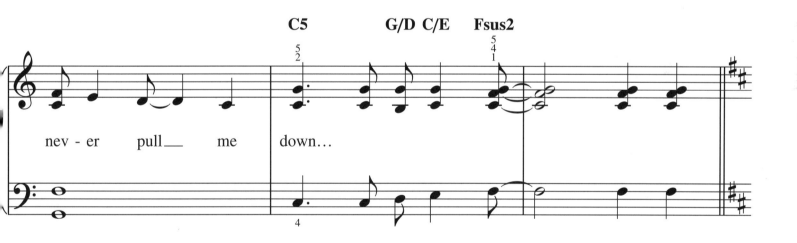

C5　　G/D C/E　Fsus2

nev - er pull__ me down...

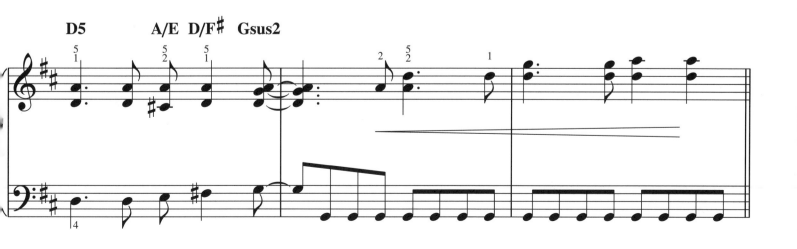

D5　　　A/E D/F#　Gsus2

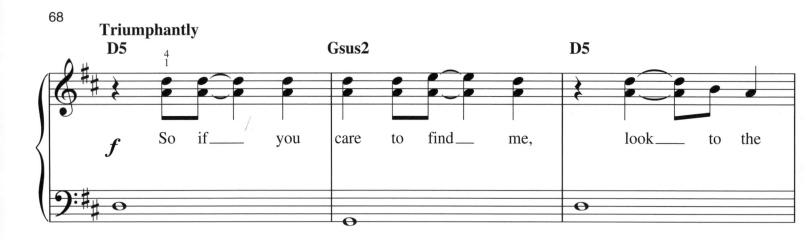

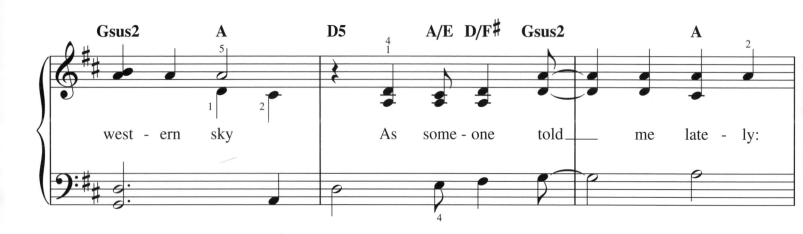

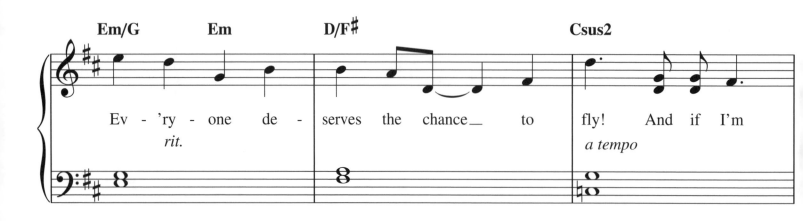

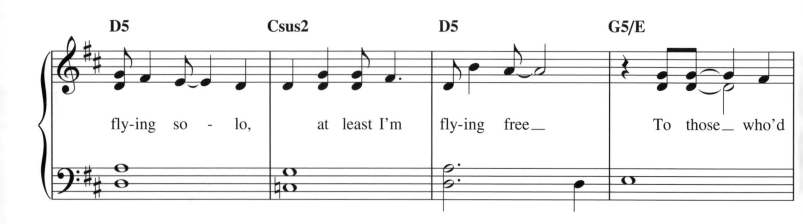

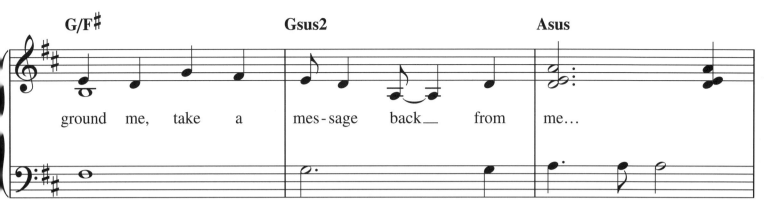

**With determination, slower**

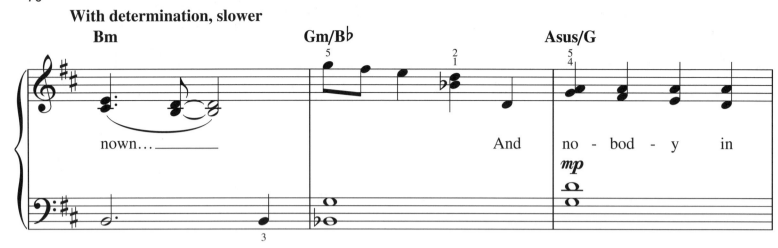

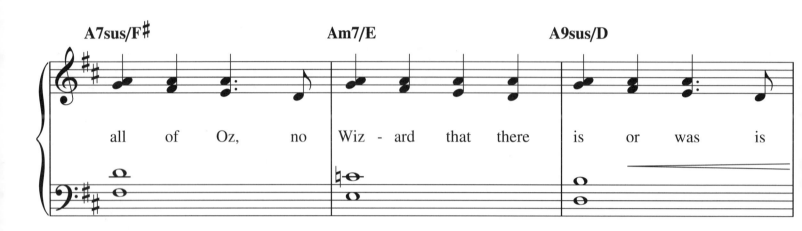

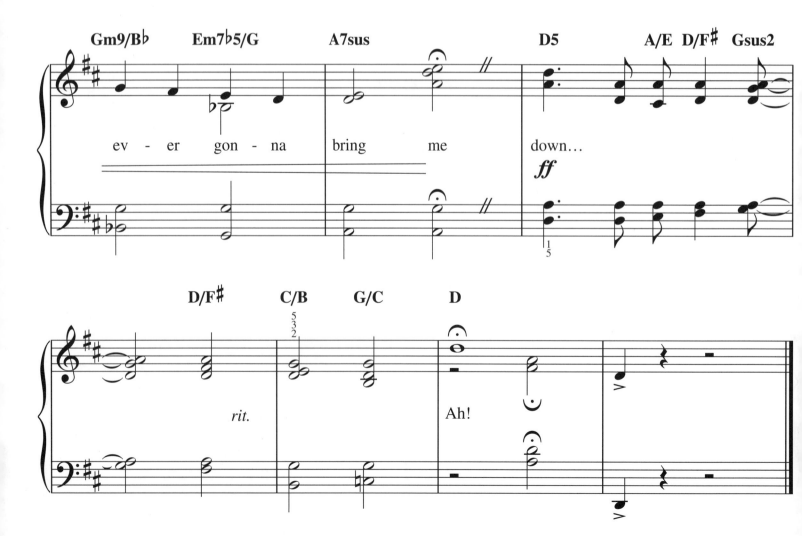

# I COULDN'T BE HAPPIER

Music and Lyrics by
STEPHEN SCHWARTZ

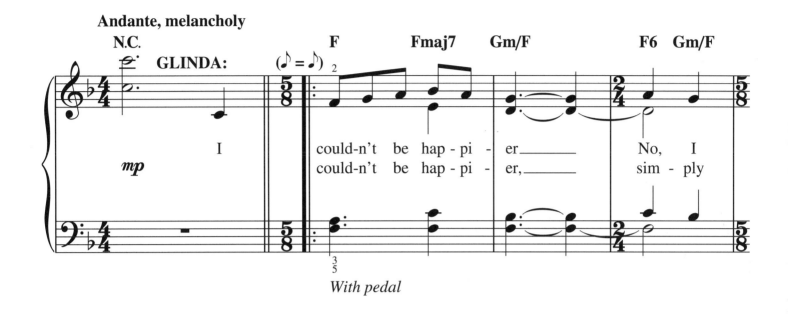

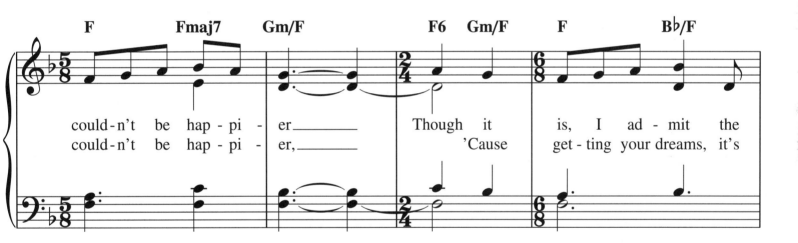

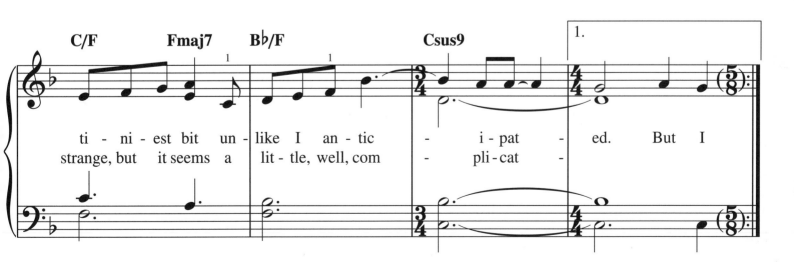

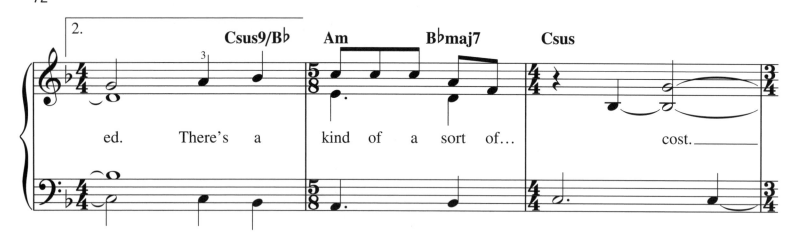

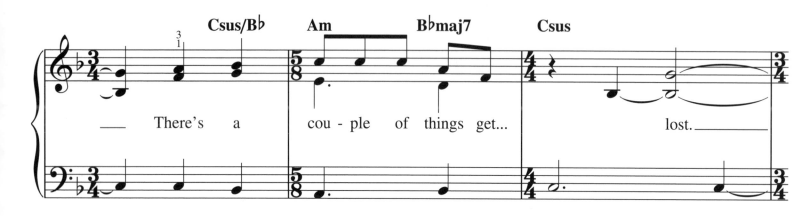

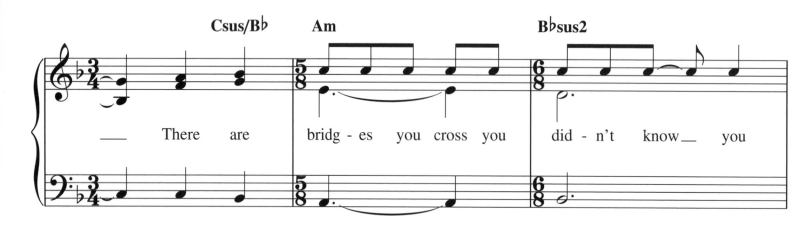

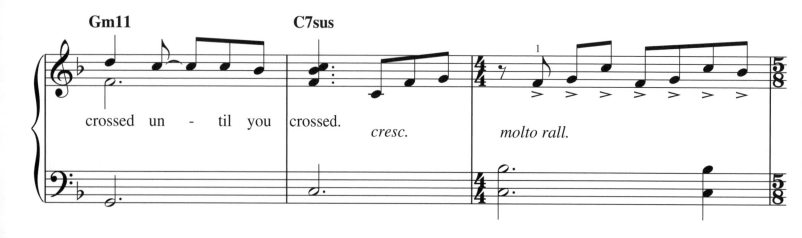

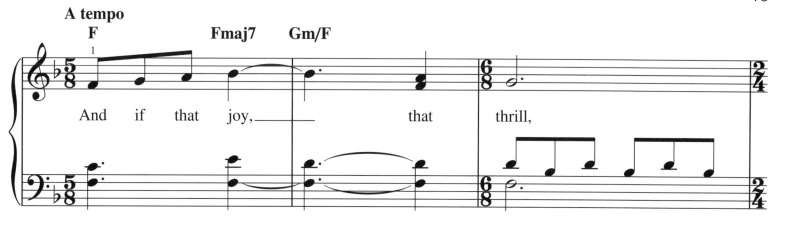

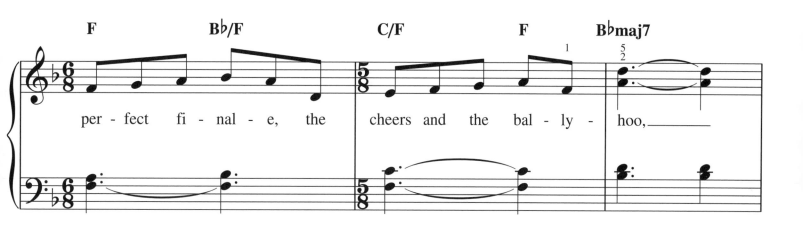

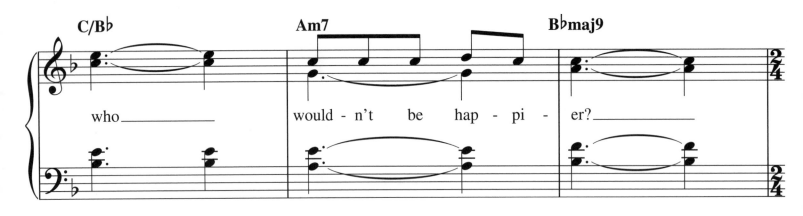

who_____ would - n't be hap - pi - er?_____

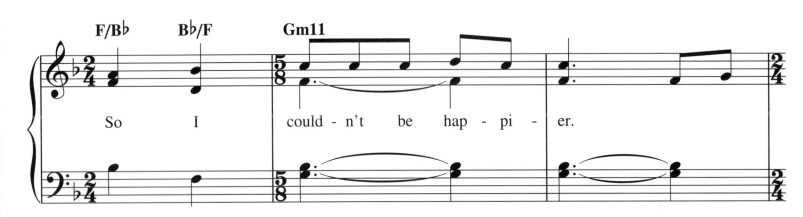

So I could - n't be hap - pi - er.

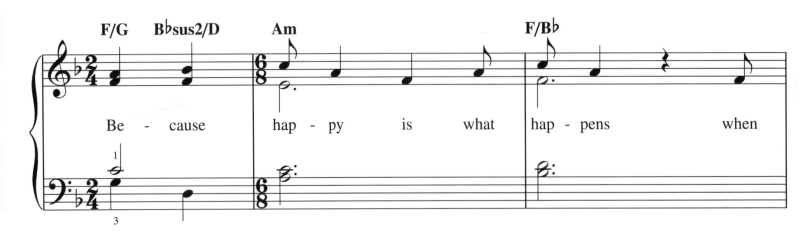

Be - cause hap - py is what hap - pens when

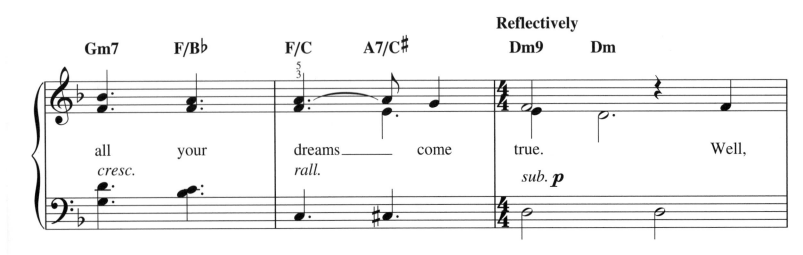

all your dreams_____ come true. Well,

*cresc.* *rall.* *sub.* **p**

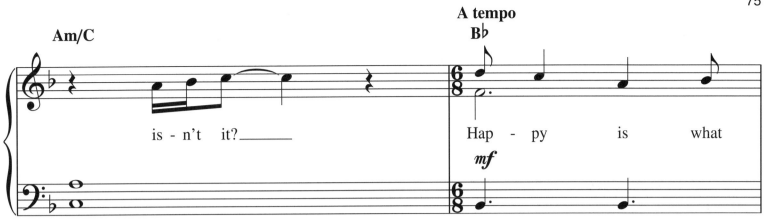

# WONDERFUL

Music and Lyrics by
STEPHEN SCHWARTZ

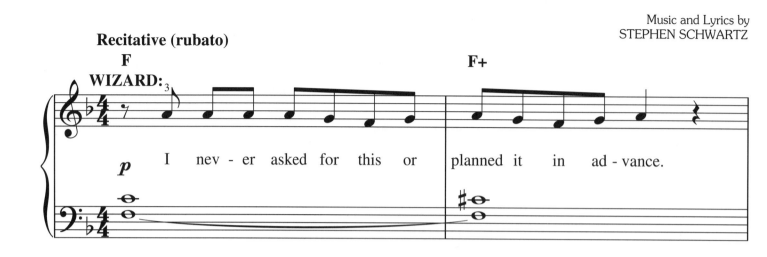

I nev-er asked for this or planned it in ad-vance.

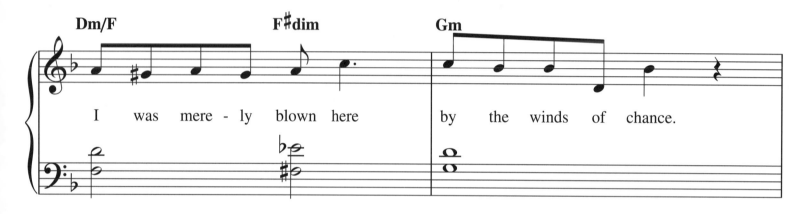

I was mere-ly blown here by the winds of chance.

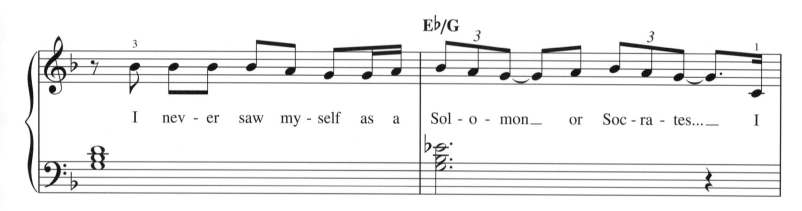

I nev-er saw my-self as a Sol-o-mon__ or Soc-ra-tes...__ I

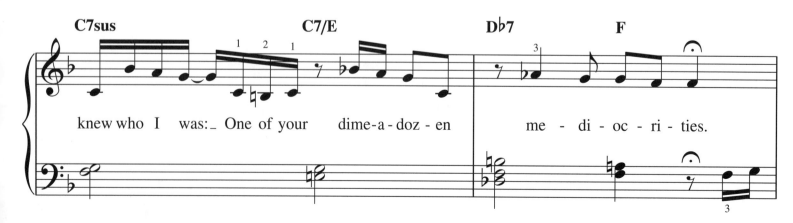

knew who I was:__ One of your dime-a-doz-en me-di-oc-ri-ties.

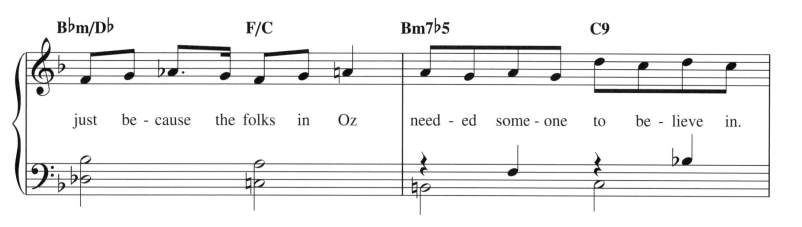

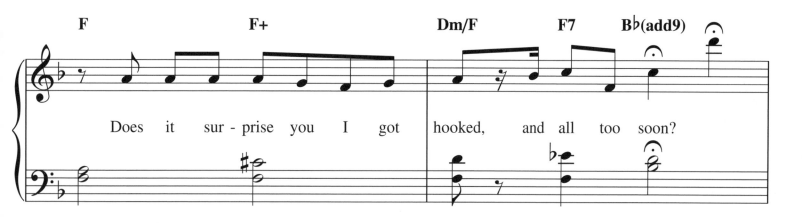

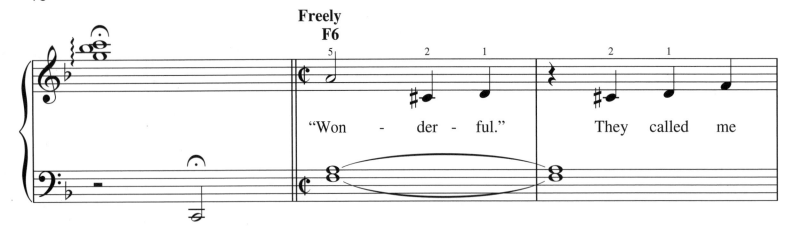

Be - lieve me, it's hard___ to re -

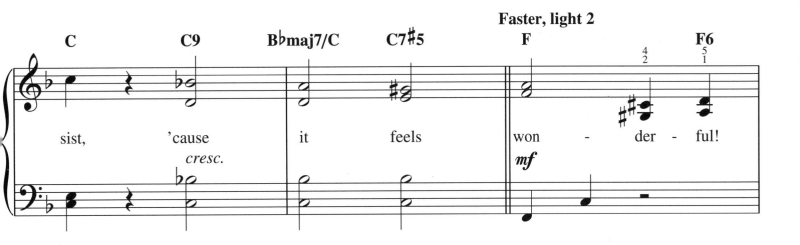

sist, 'cause it feels won - der - ful!

They think I'm won - der - ful! Hey, look who's

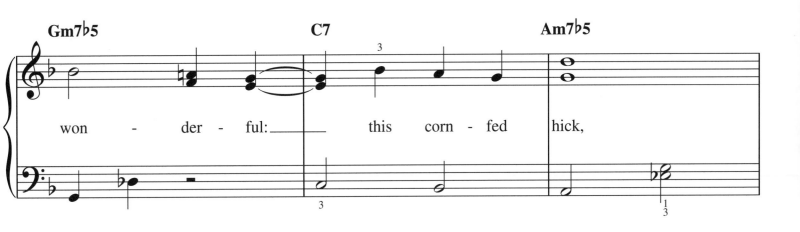

won - der - ful:___ this corn - fed hick,

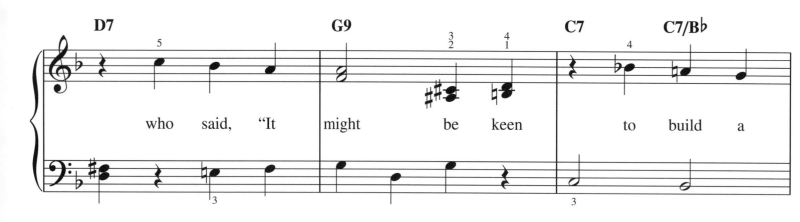

who said, "It    might    be    keen    to    build    a

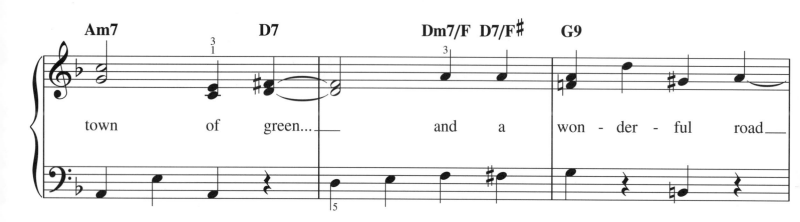

town    of    green...    and    a    won - der - ful    road

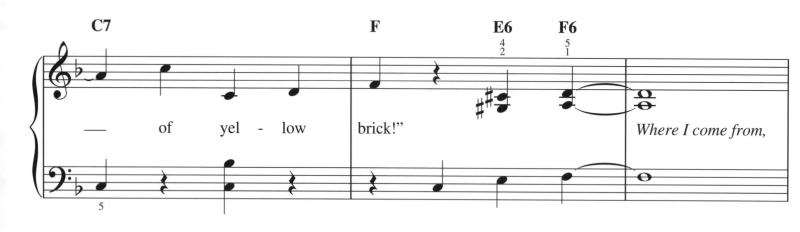

of    yel - low    brick!"    *Where I come from,*

*we believe all sorts of things that aren't true—we call it... "history."*    A

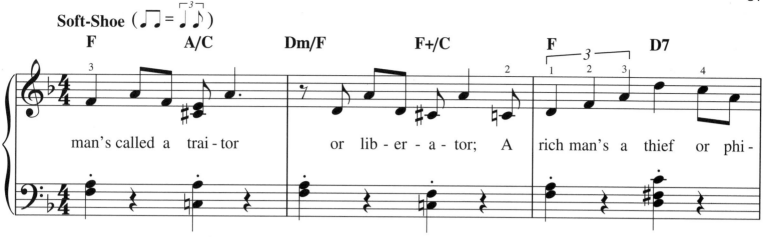

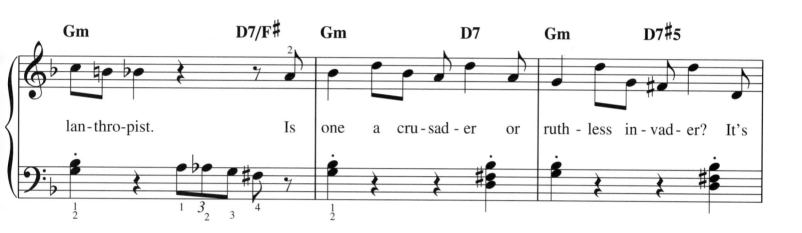

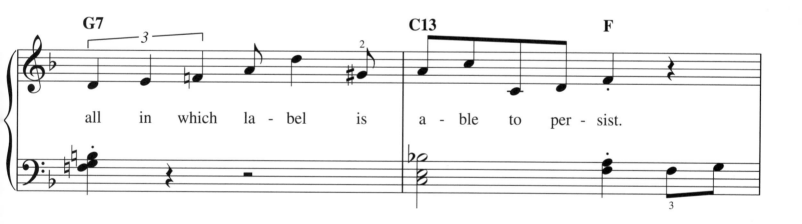

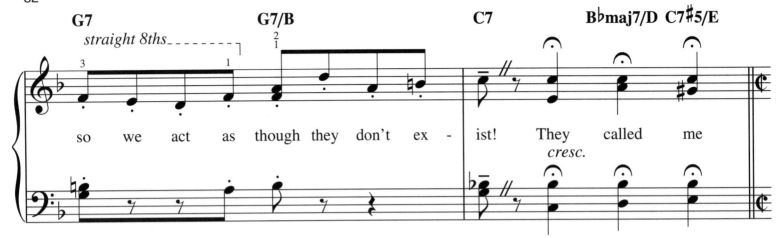

**G7** **G7/B** **C7** **B♭maj7/D C7♯5/E**

*straight 8ths*

so we act as though they don't ex - ist! They called me

*cresc.*

**Moderate Ragtime**
**F6** **G7**

won - der - ful So I *am* won - der - ful...

*f*

**Gm7♭5** **C7/B♭**

— In fact: it's so much who I am, it's part of my

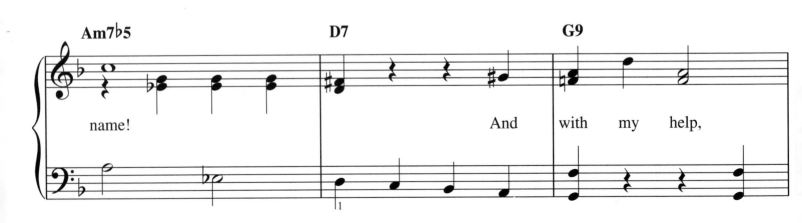

**Am7♭5** **D7** **G9**

name! And with my help,

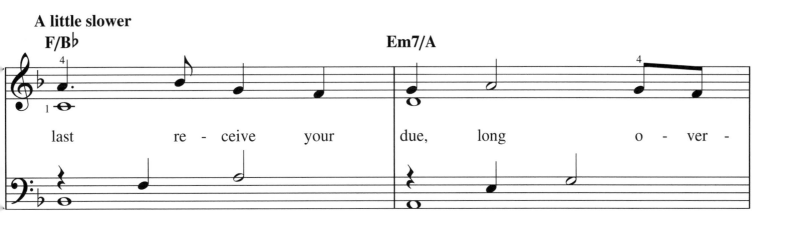

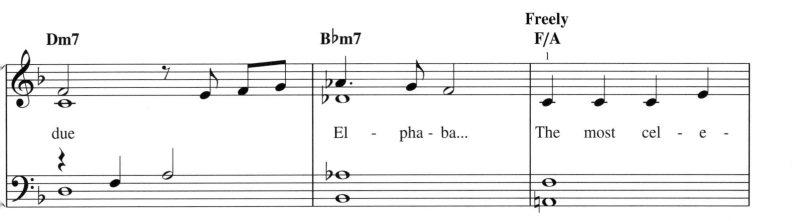

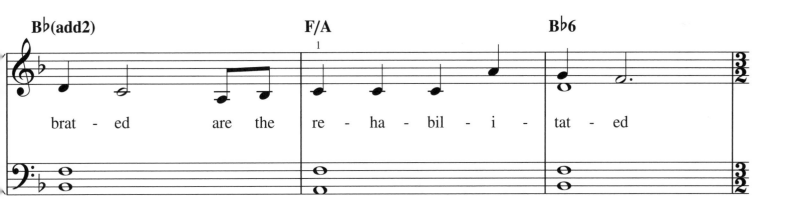

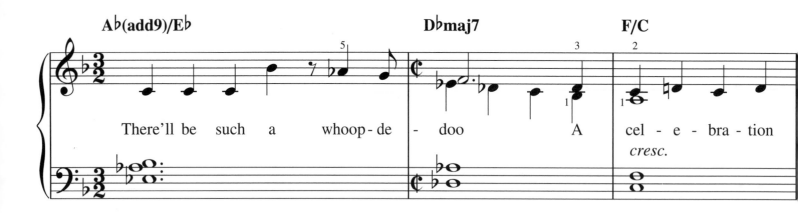

There'll be such a whoop-de - doo A cel - e - bra - tion

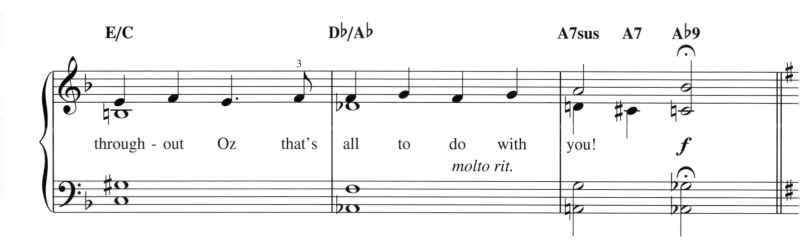

through - out Oz that's all to do with you!

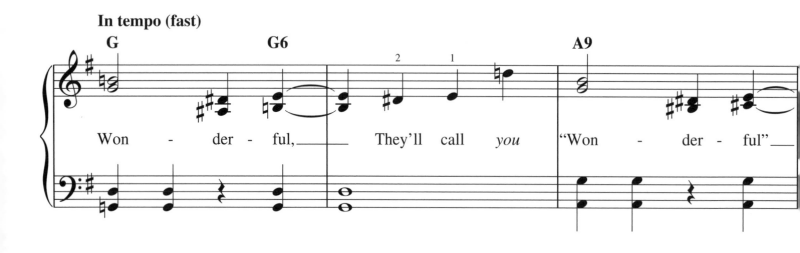

**In tempo (fast)**

Won - der - ful,___ They'll call *you* "Won - der - ful"___

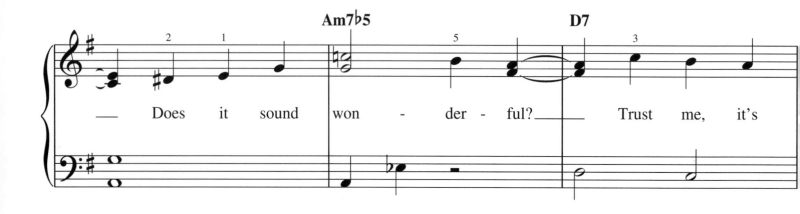

___ Does it sound won - der - ful?___ Trust me, it's

85

# AS LONG AS YOU'RE MINE

Music and Lyrics by
STEPHEN SCHWARTZ

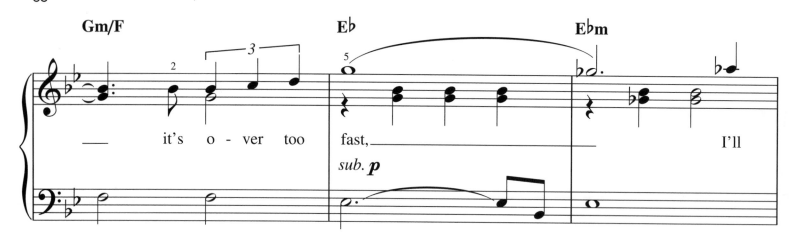

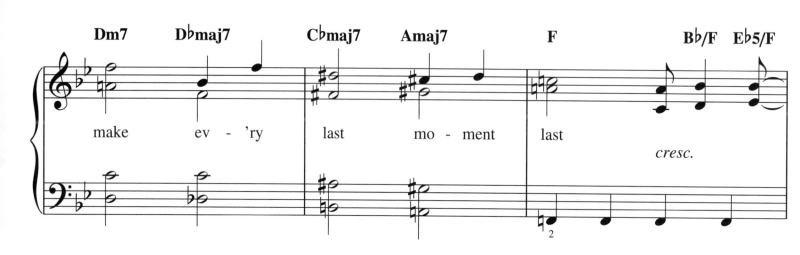

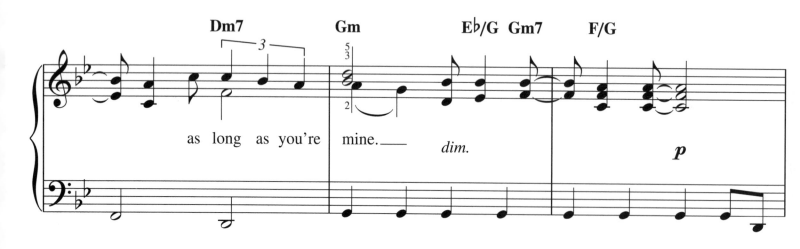

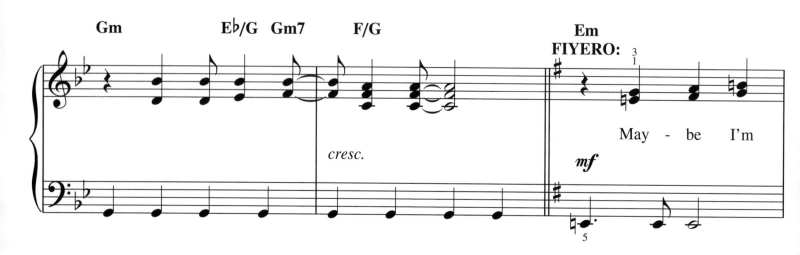

brain - less, may - be I'm wise,____ but you've got me

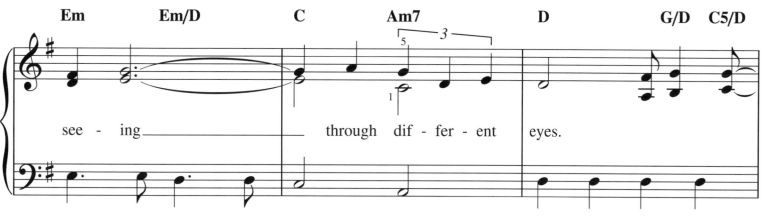

see - ing____ through dif - fer - ent eyes.

Some - how I've fall - en

un - der your spell,____ and some-how I'm feel - ing____

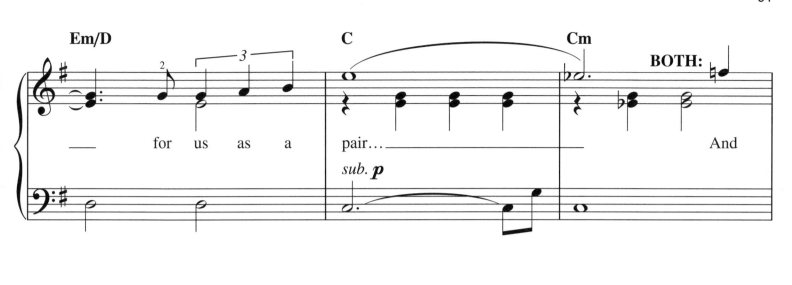

for us as a pair...... And

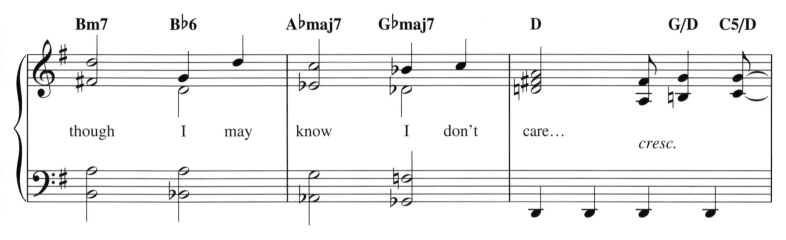

though I may know I don't care...

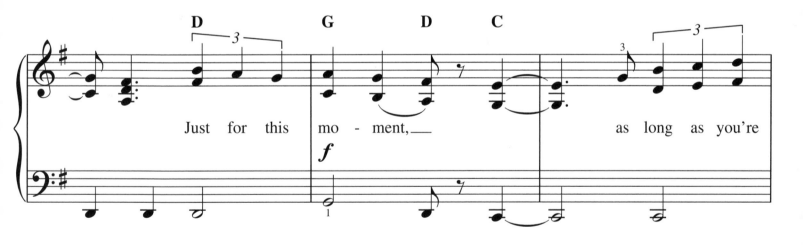

Just for this mo - ment,___ as long as you're

mine, come be how you want__ to,

as long as you're mine...

# NO GOOD DEED

Music and Lyrics by
STEPHEN SCHWARTZ

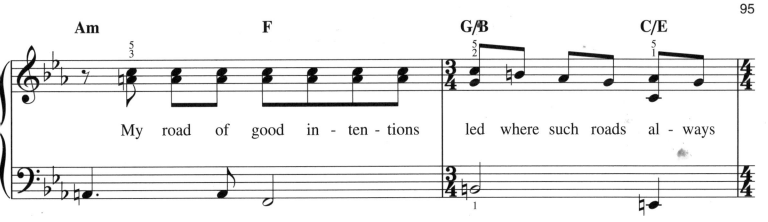

My road of good in-ten-tions led where such roads al-ways

lead.___ No good deed goes un-

pun-ished....___

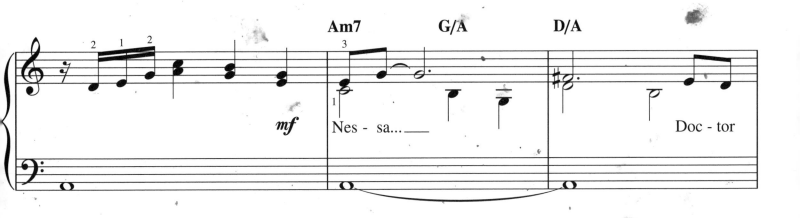

Nes-sa...___ Doc-tor

Is that all good deeds are when looked at with an ice-cold eye?

If that's all good deeds are, may-be that's the rea-son why...
cresc.

molto rall.

No good deed goes un - pun - ished__

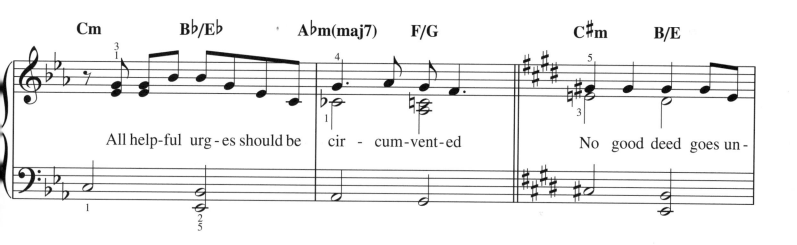

All help-ful urg-es should be cir-cum-vent-ed No good deed goes un-

pun - ished__          Sure, I meant well Well, look at          what well - meant did...____

____          All right, e - nough, so  be  it!          So  be  it

then...          Let all  of Oz be a - greed:          I'm wick - ed through and

*dim. poco rit.*          *p*

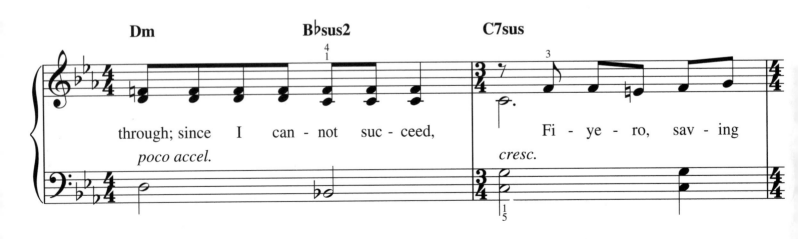

through; since  I  can - not  suc - ceed,          Fi - ye - ro, sav - ing

*poco accel.*          *cresc.*

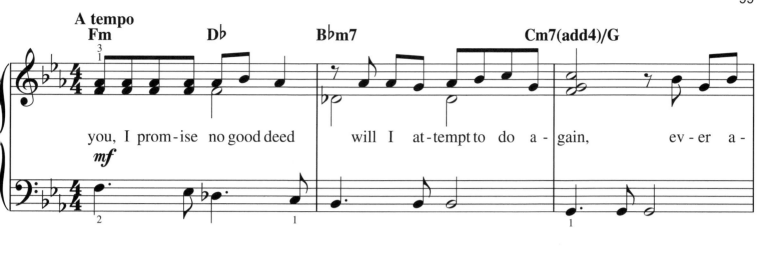

you, I prom-ise no good deed will I at-tempt to do a - gain, ev - er a-

gain... No good deed will I

do_____ a - gain!

# FOR GOOD

Music and Lyrics by
STEPHEN SCHWARTZ

help us most to grow, if we let them,___ and we

help them in re - turn. Well, I don't know if I be -

lieve that's true,___ But I know I'm who I am to - day be -

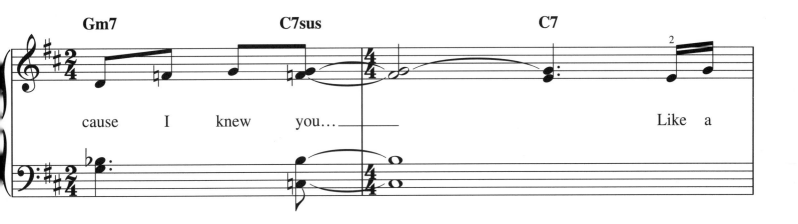

cause I knew you...___ Like a

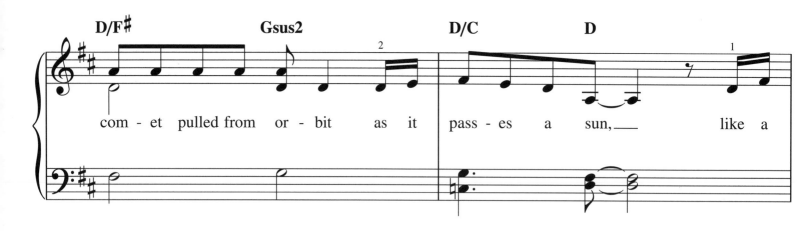

com - et pulled from or - bit as it pass - es a sun,___ like a

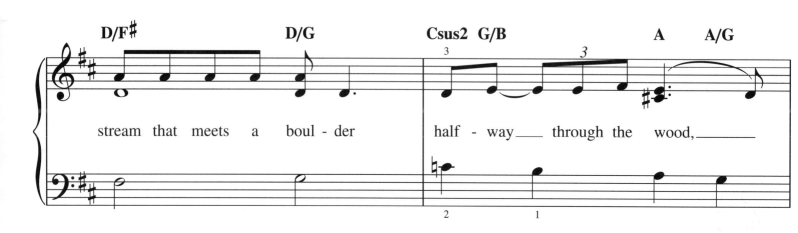

stream that meets a boul - der half - way___ through the wood,_____

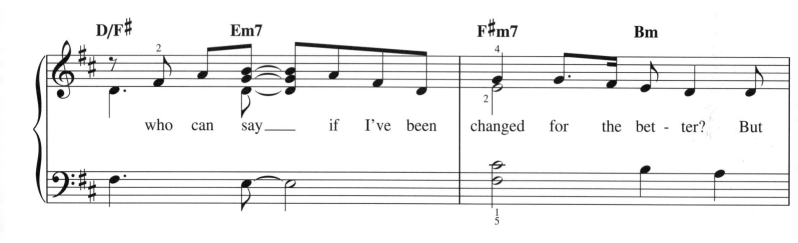

who can say___ if I've been changed for the bet - ter? But

be - cause I knew you,

what I learned from you, you'll____ be with me____ like a

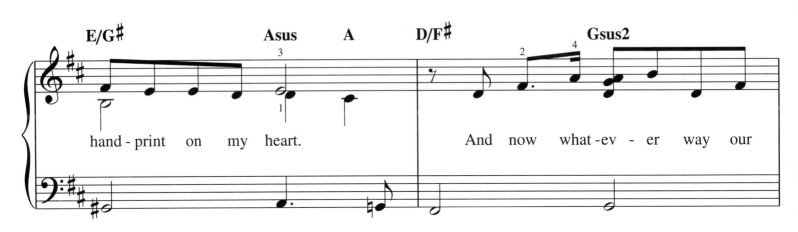

hand - print on my heart. And now what - ev - er way our

stor - ies end,____ I know you have re - writ - ten mine by

be - ing my friend.____ Like a

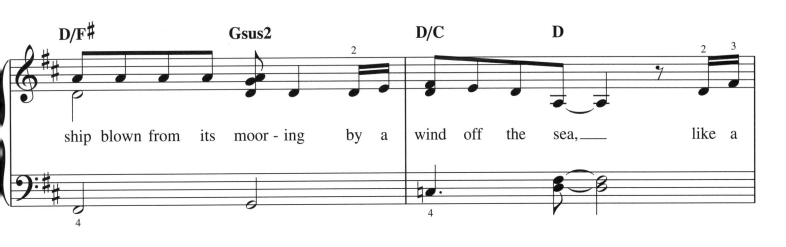

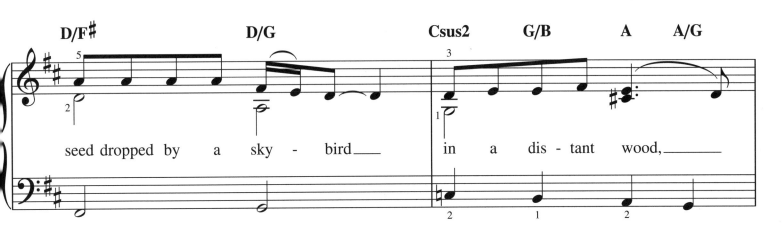

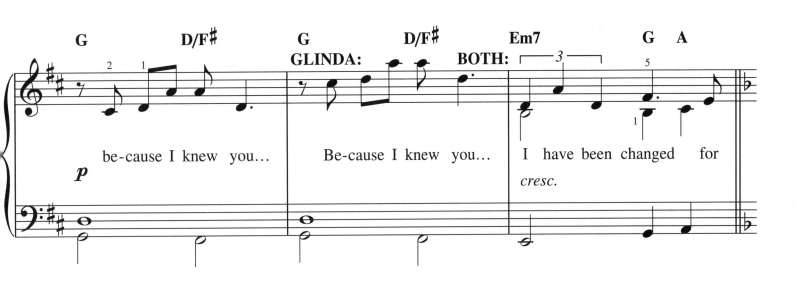

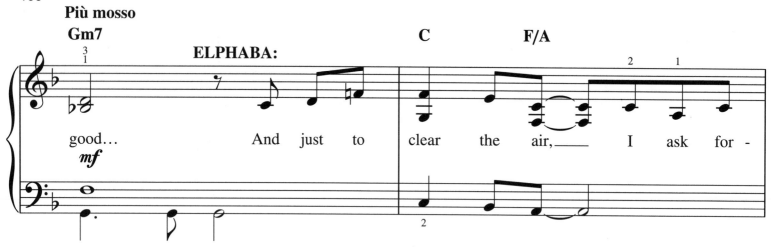

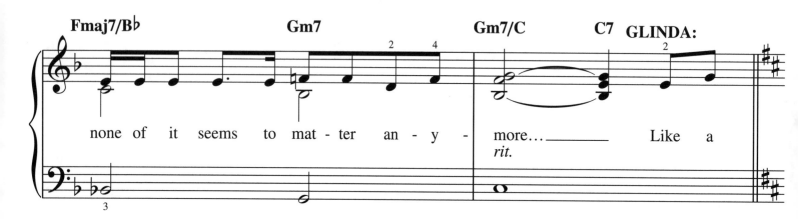

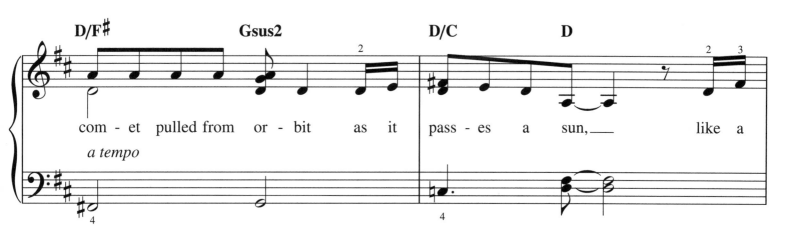

com - et pulled from or - bit as it pass - es a sun,___ like a

*a tempo*

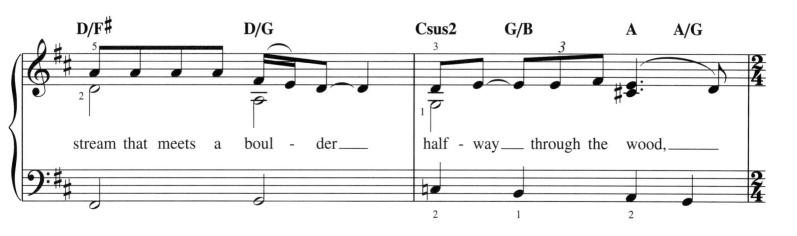

stream that meets a boul - der___ half - way__ through the wood,_____

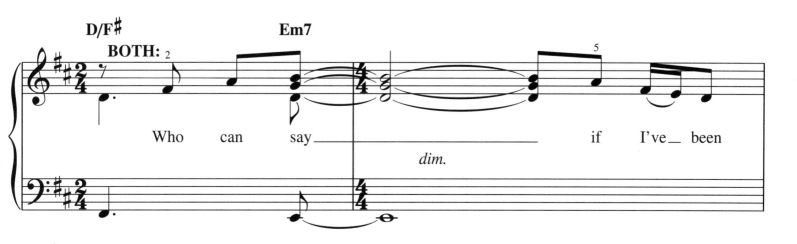

BOTH:

Who can say_____ if I've__ been

*dim.*

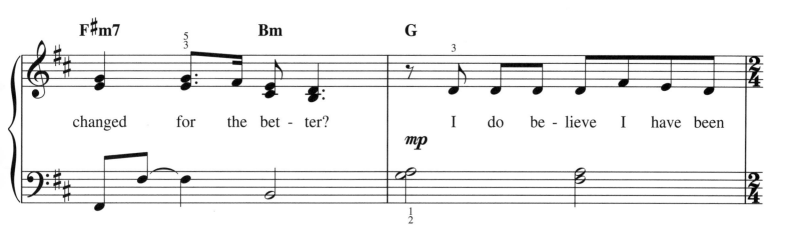

changed for the bet - ter? I do be - lieve I have been

*mp*

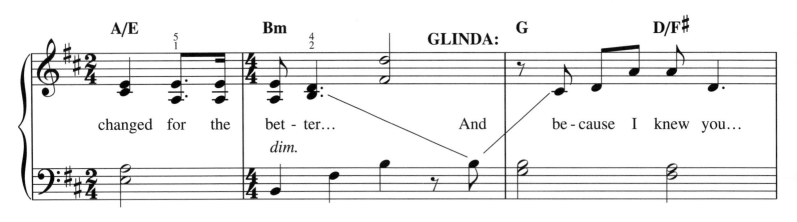

changed for the bet - ter...

And be - cause I knew you...

*dim.*

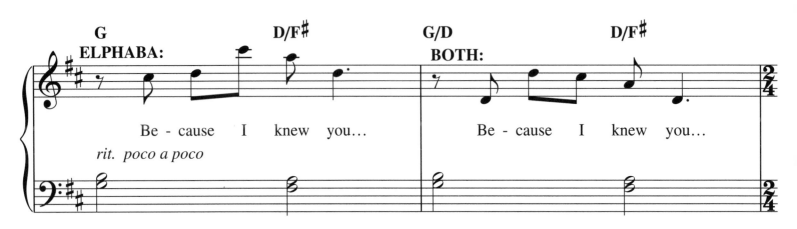

Be - cause I knew you...

Be - cause I knew you...

*rit. poco a poco*

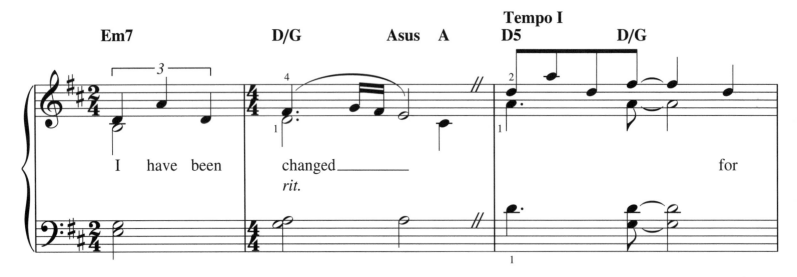

I have been changed_____ for

*rit.*

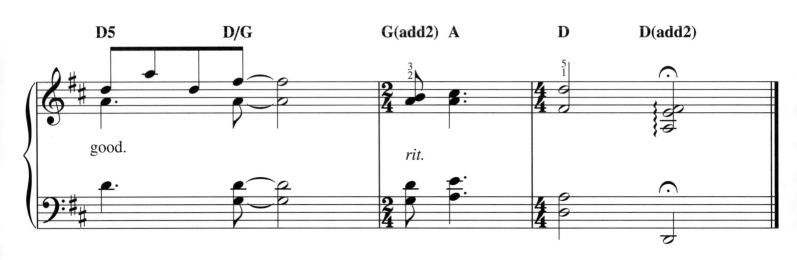

good.

*rit.*